For my son, Dylan.
I love you with all of my heart.

THIS
BETTER
WORK

A FEMALE FOUNDER'S (WILD) JOURNEY
THROUGH THE (HYPER-MASCULINE)
TECH STARTUP WORLD

LYNSIE CAMPBELL

Linda ~
Best Neighbor
ever!
♡

LIONCREST
PUBLISHING

THIS BETTER WORK
A Female Founder's (Wild) Journey through the (Hyper-Masculine) Tech Startup World

ISBN HARDCOVER: 978-1-5445-2444-3
      PAPERBACK: 978-1-5445-2442-9
      EBOOK: 978-1-5445-2443-6

CONTENTS

ACKNOWLEDGMENTS

To all of those who loved and supported me during this process, thank you.

To my mom, thank you for letting me run toward cliffs, trusting that I wouldn't throw myself over the edge, even if I came close many times. You let me carve a path that was so perfectly and painfully my own—not that I gave you any choice.

To my dad, I honestly can't believe how many times you agreed to move me across the city, state, and country. Let's be honest, though; it's your fault. I get it from you.

To my brother, Ryan, thank you for being the most entertaining uncle imaginable. Dylan has the best sense of humor thanks to you.

Speaking of the kid, enormous thanks and appreciation to Brian Arnone for being an amazing co-parent and friend.

Special thank you to Lauren Puschaver for being the best second mom my kid could've ever asked for.

To Darrin Filer, thank you for always taking me to the classiest places on my bike. And for making pancakes while I wrote this book.

Thank you to Nathaniel Minto for tolerating the long way home. And for letting me pretend that I've been your best friend for the past ten years. You've definitely been one of mine.

Thank you to Julie and Josh Vender for always having "fancy" beer in the fridge for me. Your house is my favorite pit stop.

Huge thanks to Chris and Rachel Millard for providing levity and laughs when I need them. Our kids are going to get in so much trouble together. I can't wait.

To David Evans, thank you for always answering the phone, listening, and being honest with me, even when it's 5:00 a.m. your time. I am forever grateful for everything you've done for me.

To the early ShowClix team: Nate Good, Matt Donnelly, Rob Powers, Erin (Borger) Powers, Ryan Hurst, Melinda Colaizzi, Lauren Lippello, and Tom Costa. This book would've been a million words long if I'd included *all the stories*. You made every day so much fun.

Thank you to the two people who are currently forced to spend time with me every day: Grant Gillman and Anna Lawn. No time is the wrong time for hotdoggin'.

Thank you to Ted Serbinski for believing in me when I needed it more than anything else and for becoming an amazing friend and advisor since.

Thank you to Jenny Fielding and Scott Hartley for giving me the opportunity to bring The Fund to Pittsburgh.

To Jennifer Fried, Chris Bergman, and Alejandra Rovirosa, thanks for hopping on calls every Monday to judge Ted's hair with me. I can't wait to invest in the Midwest with yinz.

And to those of you who gave me a chance early in my career: Deirdre Dod, James Avenell, Mitch Schneider, Marcee Rondan, Mark Seremet, Jim Jen, Frank Demmler, Matt Harbaugh, and Kathy Mitchell (RIP). Thank you for taking a chance on me.

Thank you to Emily Gindlesparger, Chas Hoppe, Hal Clifford, and the rest of the team at Scribe Media for giving me the process, insight, and emotional support to get from idea to finished book in a year. I truly hope it won't be the last one I write.

Huge thank you to my editor, Storms Reback (not Rick Sebak), for helping me find the best way possible to share my story.

Huge shoutouts to Christina Lee for the most amazing illustrations and Allison Braund-Harris for your support through launch.

And to all of the female founders out there, I wrote this for you. You are not alone. If you ever need anything, I'm here for you. Seriously.

INTRODUCTION

I WASN'T BORN THE right gender. I didn't come from money. I didn't go to a prestigious university. I didn't have an MBA. I never worked at Goldman Sachs. I wasn't an engineer. And I wasn't based in the right city.

I also didn't know any of this mattered when I became an entrepreneur. There were *a lot* of things I didn't know—things that I can help you navigate.

For one, the founder's journey isn't linear. There isn't a quick and straight path from point A to point B. And for female founders, the journey is filled with even more hurdles than it is for our male counterparts. Our path is and always will be curvy, chaotic, and far more unpredictable than average. There's so much we can't anticipate, and nothing is easy. We're constantly blanketed in fear, confusion, loneliness, and self-doubt. Being a founder is as volatile as the stock market and comes with only one guarantee: at times the obstacles will be so absurdly difficult they will seem almost comical.

Because of these difficulties, getting bitten by the entrepreneurial bug might seem like a cruel twist of fate, but somehow it's still the most fulfilling thing we'll ever do. Because running parallel to the chaos and loneliness and confusion is a love story. This journey isn't just about us. It's about our teams, the product, the market, and our customers. It's about building, creating, solving, and, if everything works out, celebrating.

There are lots of things I'd do differently if I could travel back in time. I'd be kinder to myself; that's for sure. I'd prioritize happiness over heartache. That's my mantra now. I learned it much too late, but you can avoid this mistake—and a bunch of others.

I'm the founder of two tech companies, ShowClix and Lane-Spotter. One was acquired. The other I burned to the ground. In between these two ventures, when I was burned out from tech, I started a dog-walking company. I scaled it from nothing to a full-blown business in three months—and it changed my life.

I feel like I've crammed about seven different lives into the forty-three years I've been alive. I've survived everything a startup can throw at you. I've done every job, survived two accelerators, raised millions of dollars in funding, and hired dozens of people. Some things I did well. Others I did not.

There's no playbook for startup life. It's a game of survival, like trying to live through a real-life zombie apocalypse. At any given moment you don't know if you're running toward salvation or away from impending doom—all the while making decisions that will have a significant impact on your future, as well as everyone around you.

Every founder makes some great decisions along the way, and every founder makes some colossal mistakes. This book is an honest, raw look at the best decisions and biggest mistakes I made along my startup journey. It's a peek into what it was like to build something from scratch as a first-time, nontechnical female founder, and I didn't do it in Silicon Valley or New York City, but in Pittsburgh. I enjoyed some tremendous highs and some equally dismal lows, and all along the way I pushed myself forward with a few hopeful words: *This better work.*

CHAPTER ONE

Getting Acquired

WHEN SHOWCLIX, THE first company I founded, was auctioned off to the highest bidder in 2017, I had conflicting feelings. It was obviously an exciting moment, but because I'd walked away from the company in 2015, I was forced to watch from the sidelines.

The sale was a private equity play. Two firms were interested in ShowClix, and both had the same idea: acquire the best technology in the event space and roll up the middle market. The industry was ripe for this—had been for years. So many small companies were competing for the same clients. None of us were going to win alone.

I had no idea what the outcome of this transaction would be—for the company or the people who built it. Tom Costa, who'd become ShowClix's CEO in 2013 after being COO for four years, was my go-between during the sale. While I always believed that Tom had my best interest at heart, I couldn't stop wondering, *Are Jonathan and Clive going to try to fuck me over again?*

One of my main frustrations with Jonathan and Clive was that they didn't understand or acknowledge all the hard work we'd done before they showed up. In their minds, ShowClix didn't exist before they got to the party. What they didn't realize is that they *crashed* the party. They were the guys who showed up drunk, puked in the sink, and ruined it for everyone.

They didn't care about the bootstrapping, the credit card debt, or the sweat equity. They saw no value in any of it. They had no idea what it was like to build something from scratch or to take a $30,000-per-year pay cut to make sure their company had a chance of surviving.

Neither of them had put their heart and soul into a business only to end up divorced, depressed, starved, and broken. These guys were the opposite of "founder-friendly." They weren't mentors or advisors or coaches. They were simply a source of capital and, more often than not, adversaries.

Don't get me wrong. There are plenty of investors out there who are great mentors and advisors—investors who have lived the life, can relate to your struggles, and are genuinely helpful. I just never had a chance to work with any of them.

Yet here I was, considered one of the "lucky ones." The tech company I'd started was being acquired. A decade of incredible successes (and the occasional epic fuckup) had culminated in this moment. Very few founders make it this far. For an entrepreneur, selling your first company is supposed to be the epitome of success, a dream come true, but I disliked my investors so much that I wasn't able to enjoy the moment. I should've been excited. I should've been proud. Instead, I was shocked. And I was fucking pissed.

To help me through the acquisition, I hired a delightful veteran startup attorney named Steve Cherin. He'd earned a reputation for going to bat for the new crop of female tech founders who had started to emerge in Pittsburgh, such as Priya Amin from Flexable and Leah Lizarondo from 412 Food Rescue. While reviewing the paperwork, we found a sentence in the disclosures schedule that spoke volumes about the investors' attitude toward me and my co-founder:

> *The Company has outstanding loans to Lynsie Camuso and Joshua Dziabiak ("Founder Loans") aggregating $71,706 for both persons.*

They didn't even bother to get my name right. I'd been divorced for seven years and had taken back my maiden name (Campbell) long ago.

As galling as this was, it didn't come out of nowhere. When Josh and I were formalizing the company in 2006, our attorney recommended that we create an LLC, and we followed his advice. When we obtained our series A investment in 2009, the lead investor insisted that we convert to a C-corp, so we did.

When Josh and I were filing our taxes the following year, we discovered that the conversion from LLC to C-corp had left us owing more than $70,000 to the government—*personally*. Neither of us had that kind of money. It was a financial burden that would've crippled us, so we asked for help and, luckily, got it. The series A investors agreed that our company ShowClix, not Josh and I, would pay the taxes. Assuming it was case closed, Josh and I never thought about it or talked about it again—until we sold the company eight years later.

I was livid and perplexed. Why were they even bothering with this? Why not let it go? These guys had offended me numerous times over the years, but this was the biggest slap in the face to date. They clearly didn't value all the sacrifices we'd made to build the company. They never cared about us as founders or as people. All they cared about was getting every last dollar they possibly could. I'll never understand how some people can think they're helping a company grow while surgically removing the heart and soul of the business at the same time.

There was no chance in hell I was going to sell my company with this in the agreement. Nope. No way. Fuck that.

A protracted back-and-forth began. My lawyer sent a note to Jonathan and Clive, telling them that I didn't recall ever agreeing to repay the $70,000 "loan" and asking if they had any notes or documentation.

Even after admitting that they didn't have any "underlying documentation," they kept pushing.

And I pushed back. I wasn't going to sign the acquisition documents until this issue was resolved. Period.

After a few more days of tense negotiations that threatened to delay (or possibly even cancel) the close of the deal, the investors caved, agreeing to write off the loans and remove the request from the disclosures schedule.

I sent one last email to my attorney, thanking him for his help. "I know that loan amount wasn't a lot," I told him, "but it was about more than the money for me."

It didn't feel great having to fight so hard to remove a sentence from a document, a sentence that never should have been added in the first place, but I was thankful that the saga was over. I couldn't wait to light the match and set the bridge I'd just crossed on fire. I never wanted to talk to Jonathan and Clive again. One of the worst periods of my time in the tech startup world was finally behind me. I would never have to experience anything that was so stressful and humiliating ever again.

Or so I thought.

CHAPTER TWO

Chasing Dreams

I'VE BEEN CHASING dreams my whole life.

When I was a kid, my parents let me try lots of stuff. I took violin and piano lessons. I sucked at both. I ran track and cross country. Played soccer and softball. I was athletic, but it wasn't "my thing." None of these things were my thing.

I found solace in the arts and media. I read a ton of books and listened to a lot of music, but I loved writing more than anything else. Two English teachers at my small high school just outside of Pittsburgh helped nurture my love of language. Mrs. Herb picked transformational books for me to read and encouraged my writing. Mr. Sullivan was in charge of the school's new media club, which was made possible by Channel One News, the daily news program for teenagers that was founded in 1989. Channel One provided audiovisual equipment to any schools that aired its programming.

I loved Channel One. Anderson Cooper and Lisa Ling both started their long and distinguished careers in journalism there. Kids who were not much older than me were covering the news. I wanted to do the same, so I signed up to write, produce, and direct our high school morning news program, Raidervision. I hosted the program a few times a week with my friend Dave English. I'd finally found my thing.

I was a rabid consumer of media, mostly books, movies, and music. I learned who I was by way of Kurt Vonnegut, Depeche Mode, Winona Ryder, *True Romance*, George Orwell, and R.E.M. My unabashed love of these things led to a series of jobs that indulged my interests.

I grew up in a middle-class household where the collars were more blue than white. My dad worked at Wendy's and drove buses for Greyhound before he landed a stable job as a deputy sheriff for Allegheny County. My mom was a bookkeeper for my rich uncle but has probably never made more than $40,000 a year in her life. I knew in high school that I was going to need a job, but I didn't want just any old job. I wanted a job I actually liked. I still feel this way today.

When I was fifteen, I started working at the local video store, Video Hits. I organized the VHS tapes on the shelves, ate fistfuls of popcorn, and made small talk with the people who'd come to find their evening escape. Bonus: I also got unlimited free video rentals.

After a few years at Video Hits, I upgraded from VHS to the big screen and started working at a movie theater. The screen might have been bigger, but the benefits were nearly the same. I continued to eat an unhealthy amount of popcorn and watch any movie I wanted to see for free.

I went to college at Penn State University, and when I came home in the summers, I worked at Barnes & Noble, where I alphabetized books, worked the register, and made lattes at the in-house Starbucks. The benefits were now more adult: discounted books and free coffee.

Soon after arriving in State College, Pennsylvania, I declared my major. I was going to study journalism—the perfect major for those who are curious and love to write. I honed my interviewing, research, and writing skills. I learned how to edit audio and video. I thrived under the pressure of a deadline. I never would've guessed that this humanities-based major would be such a good primer for entrepreneurship.

My first internship during college was at KDKA-TV, the CBS affiliate in Pittsburgh. I worked at the assignments desk for a guy named Dicky Nassar. He sent me out with photographers to cover minor events. I'd talk to the people involved, collect details, and report back to Dicky. I spent my nights calling the local police departments and gathering the same sort of information.

I enjoyed the experience so much that for my next internship I researched and applied to a bunch of different programs in television. Most of them were in New York City. That seemed more doable to me than Los Angeles. In retrospect I'm not sure why my nineteen-year-old self thought *either* was doable.

I applied to *The Today Show, Good Morning America, Dateline, Late Night with David Letterman,* and *Late Night with Conan O'Brien*—all the usual suspects at the time. A few weeks later, my phone rang. It was the HR manager from *The Rosie O'Donnell Show.* She wanted me to come in for an interview. A week later, my dad drove me to New York City. It was cold, and traffic was horrible. He grumbled the entire time, but I knew he was excited too. Two weeks later, I got the call I was hoping for. The internship was mine if I wanted it.

Holy shit, I was moving to New York City to work at *The Rosie O'Donnell Show!*

The only downside: it was an *unpaid* internship. My parents agreed to cover the cost of an apartment equal to what I would have been paying in State College. I took a bus into Manhattan from North Jersey every morning. I had a cell phone, but there was no GPS at the time. I have no sense of direction, so I was constantly lost.

The Rosie O'Donnell Show accepted seven interns at a time. We rotated through departments, learning about each aspect of the business and meeting everyone who worked on the show. First, I worked with the producers. Then I was sent to the talent department, which was responsible for booking guests.

On my first day in the talent department, I said hello to the four associates with whom I'd be working. I hadn't finished my second sentence before James Avenell, the show's most senior talent booker, stopped me and said, "Are you from Pittsburgh?"

Wow, it had taken him almost no time to pick up on my yinzer accent. "I am."

"Very cool. My partner is from Pittsburgh. His parents own the James Street Tavern on the North Side."

And just like that, I was completely at ease.

A few weeks after I'd started working in the talent department, the senior music producer fired her assistant. I don't know why James went out on a limb for me—the Pittsburgh connection?—but he did. He approached the senior music producer, Deirdre Dod, and the head of the talent department and told them they should give me a chance, that I worked hard and played nice with others. Deirdre agreed to give me a shot. As a talent assistant, I'd be helping her book guests and coordinating their segments.

I felt like it was the best job on the entire show. I pinched myself constantly. After dropping out of Penn State and moving to New York City, I became the youngest employee at *The Rosie O'Donnell Show*. I was twenty-one years old and working in Rockefeller Center, on the same floor as *Saturday Night Live*. I was booking the biggest musical acts in the world at the time, including N'Sync, Britney Spears, Backstreet Boys, and Christina Aguilera. Elton John once kissed me on the cheek, for fuck's sake! It was an incredible experience.

As the show was coming to an end in 2002, I knew I needed to figure out what to do next. I loved New York City, but if I didn't finish college now, I never would. I didn't want to go back to Penn State. All my college friends had graduated. So I went home to Pittsburgh, finished college at Duquesne University, and started looking around for my next gig.

Pittsburgh is one of the country's most prominent sports towns, so I grew up a sports fan. If I couldn't work in the entertainment industry, sports was a solid second option. I sent emails, with my résumé attached, to the Steelers, Penguins, and Pirates.

The Pirates called. The organization needed seasonal help in marketing and promotions. Score! Which, sadly, is not something the Pirates did a lot that season. They lost 103 games. It was *brutal*.

During my time with the Pirates, I worked closely with the Pittsburgh media. That's how I met Ryan Camuso, the morning show producer for *The Alan Cox Radio Show*, which aired on the city's alternative rock station. We got married four years after we met. Ryan had always wanted to work in television, and after being in Pittsburgh for two years, I longed to do something different. I missed the entertainment industry, so I suggested we move to Los Angeles. He agreed to give it a shot.

We had no idea what we'd do once we got there. We picked an apartment sight unseen. We had no clue what the neighborhood we would be living in was like. I'd been to Los Angeles *once* before we hopped in the car and headed west.

I landed at The Mitch Schneider Organization (MSO), a boutique music publicity firm founded by the former *Rolling Stone* journalist. I'd met MSO's vice president Marcee Rondan when I was a talent assistant at *The Rosie O'Donnell Show* and she was the Backstreet Boys' publicist. I was starting to see how this business *really* worked, that more often than not it was *who* you knew, not *what*. Just a few months after I started working at MSO, Mitch offered me a job as his assistant. Yes, please! Among my duties was assisting Mitch with his client roster, which consisted of the company's biggest clients (and some of the biggest musical acts in the world), including David Bowie, Fleetwood Mac, Tom Petty, Alanis Morrisette, Matchbox 20, and Johnny Rotten.

Ryan and I settled into life in Los Angeles as well as two kids from Western Pennsylvania could. I liked LA, but I didn't *love* it the way I'd loved New York. I felt like I spent half my life trapped in a car on a sprawling freeway. I missed the change of seasons, and I despised the elitism.

On top of all that, we were broke. Breaking news: unless you're A-list talent, working in the entertainment industry does not pay well. I paid my car insurance with a credit card for an entire year. I don't recommend doing that. Ryan and I survived by selling the CDs we'd collected through various jobs over the years. A guy would show up at our apartment in Valley Village and pay us in cash so we could cover rent.

Two years in Los Angeles was enough. It was time to head home to Pittsburgh. After two stints in major cities working in the entertainment industry, I had no idea what I was going to do now. Without a ton of options available, I returned to my roots—television. I reached out to the local CBS, ABC, and NBC affiliate stations. WPXI-TV, the NBC affiliate, hired me to help produce a series of commercials called "Stand Up, And Tell 'Em You're From Pittsburgh."

As the project was ending, the station manager approached me. "We need someone to cover as web producer while Julie is out on maternity leave. Can you do it?"

I had no business saying yes to this. I had no idea what Julie did. "Sure!" I said.

I figured I'd figure it out. I taught myself basic HTML and learned to update the website. I stayed on top of breaking news, wrote fast, and got competitive about posting stories before the other local stations did.

Working as the web producer at WPXI-TV introduced me to a side of the internet I hadn't experienced before. I'd always been a consumer, never a creator. Now I was a distributor of information on a very large scale. The reach was massive. I could feel it. I immediately became obsessed.

I decided to chase a new dream. I was going to work in tech.

CHAPTER THREE

Meeting Josh

I FOUND A JOB at Spreadshirt, a web-based custom t-shirt company based in Leipzig, Germany. The company had recently opened an office in Pittsburgh after hiring a local CEO. My job was to run marketing in the United States. As I settled into the role, I quickly realized that I needed to hire someone who could focus on all things design—and maybe wear a few other hats too.

We worked out of a tiny office on Fort Pitt Boulevard in downtown Pittsburgh. There were just four of us in the office, and half were engineers. The office was quiet. Too quiet. I'm not a quiet person, so I was hoping to hire someone who would not only do awesome work but also add some energy to the team.

I'd interviewed a handful of people before Joshua Dziabiak showed up. He was so much different than everyone else I'd discussed the job with. Part of a very religious family, he'd grown up on a twenty-acre farm near Freedom, Pennsylvania, that he referred to as the "compound." Because his family owned and operated a septic-pumping business, he liked to tell people that his family "pumped shit" for a living.

When he was fourteen, Josh convinced his parents to get him a computer and an internet connection. He then designed and built a website for himself. Before he knew it, he was building websites for local businesses in Beaver County, charging them a few hundred bucks per design. Then he'd refer them to someone else for web hosting. At some point, a lightbulb went off in his head and he asked himself, *Why am I sending all of this hosting business to somebody else? This is where the real money is.* Josh is a smart guy.

He bought a few servers and started a web hosting company called MediaCatch. He quickly grew the company and then sold it to a guy in Canada for more than a million dollars. He hadn't even turned eighteen yet. Like I said, smart. And resourceful. And very funny. He had a great sense of humor.

On my recommendation, Spreadshirt hired him, and as soon as his stuff hit his desk, I asked him to join me for a coffee and a chat. We clicked immediately. I still haven't met anyone else who I've connected with like that. I remember thinking, as we walked back to the office, that he and I were going to be tight. I knew he was going to be a big part of my life; I just had no idea what that meant yet.

Josh and I worked really well together from the outset. Conversation and ideas flowed seamlessly and endlessly. Our main goal at Spreadshirt was to get more people to open up shops, create merchandise, and sell it online. Who sells a lot of merch? Bands. Where did bands introduce themselves to the world in 2006? Myspace. Josh and I created a set of marketing campaigns that promoted Spreadshirt to small indie bands on Myspace. It worked like a charm. Within six months, we'd increased user acquisition by more than 200 percent. We proved we could get results together. And we had a ton of fun doing it.

During the first few weeks we shared an office, we swapped backstories. We talked about where we'd come from and where we wanted to go. We bonded over our love of music, pop culture, and over-the-top episodes of *Dateline NBC*. I was twenty-eight. He was eighteen. But the age gap between us was barely noticeable. I've always believed that you have a biological age and an inner age. I may be forty-three years old according to my driver's license, but if you ask me, I will forever be twenty-three. Meanwhile, Josh was a sixty-year-old Black woman. He loved Oprah Winfrey so much that for years he kept a photo of her on his nightstand next to his bed.

As we grew closer, Josh told me about an idea he had for a website that would help people find local events. He wanted the events' organizers to be able to sell tickets as well. Josh hired a software development company (a.k.a. a dev shop) in India and built a first version of the website, which gave me a good sense of where he was going with his idea. The more we talked about it, the more ideas we started to generate. I was excited. I really thought we could make this work.

Our level of commitment was the same—insanely high. We talked on the phone every morning on the way to work. During those "morning briefings," we reviewed the work we'd done overnight, discussed our plan for the day, and brainstormed new ideas. We created a second language so we could talk about our business during the day without anybody at Spreadshirt knowing that was what we were discussing. After spending the day working for Spreadshirt, we'd head over to a coffee shop on the South Side to work on our company, ShowClix.

The entrepreneurial bug that had bitten me didn't come completely out of the blue. My uncle through marriage, Nick Kratsa, was one of three brothers who'd grown up in poverty in Verona, Pennsylvania. His father, affectionately known as Billy K, carried a lunch box to his job at Edgewater Steel every morning. That wasn't his only job, though. Before heading to the steel mill, he'd wake my Uncle Nick and his brother Perry at four o'clock so they could help him deliver bread to make ends meet.

When my Uncle Nick was in high school, his dad opened a bar in Verona called Billy K's. They used the money they made from the bar to buy a hotel across the river in Harmar Township called The Red Raven. Despite having never gone to college, my Uncle Nick transformed this initial investment into a portfolio of fifteen hotels across the region, which he sold for $350 million in 2014. I'd watched somebody create a multimillion-dollar business from scratch, and that's all it takes to know that it's possible.

Josh and I spent months researching, writing, designing, and building. Neither of us was an engineer, so we had to pay for engineering. We hired a dev shop in Crimea, Ukraine, to build the minimum viable product (MVP) to test our idea and the assumptions we'd been making up to that point. I only mention the shop's location because Justin Timberlake's "Cry Me a River" was released around the same time. This created a problem for two people who took every joke way too far.

We bootstrapped the development, each of us throwing in a couple hundred bucks every week. Josh rebranded and redesigned the website while I pulled together everything needed to create an actual business and raise a round of funding. ShowClix was never going to be a side project. We were building a high-growth tech company. Spreadshirt showed us this was possible. If the weirdos who ran Spreadshirt could build a tech company and raise money, Josh and I could do the same.

I wrote a thirty-six-page business plan for a business plan competition. This seems comical to me now; no startup does this. That said, there were benefits to the exercise. To get to the point where we had a thirty-six-page business plan sitting in front of us, Josh and I talked through every last detail of the company: how we wanted it to grow, how fast we wanted it to grow, and what we wanted our team to look like while we grew. By the end of the process, there was no doubt we were on the same page.

Next, we developed a plan for launch. The live events market was big. So was the country. We decided the best way to launch a meaningful first version was to segment the market. There were a couple of ways we could do this. We could build a database focused on an initial set of cities—for example, Pittsburgh, New York, Chicago, and Miami—and add as many events as possible in those cities. Or we could focus on a specific type of event and launch across the entire country. We chose the latter, and we picked live music.

It made sense to start there. I'd spent the early part of my career in the music industry, and Josh loved the space. In fact, after he sold his first company, he tried to launch a digital record label. It didn't work out, but he maintained his love of the music industry.

The engineers we'd hired built a tool we could use to scrape any band's Myspace page and add its tour dates to our database. One of Josh's cousins, as well as one of mine, pitched in and helped out, running the bot and cleaning up any information that wasn't imported correctly. I also did this *every single night* before bed. I wanted us to hit our goal of having seven thousand concerts in our database as fast as possible. I can't remember how we landed on that number, but once we did it was absolute. As soon as we had seven thousand shows in the database, the website would go live.

We prepped to raise money. We weren't the typical startup founders you'd find in Pittsburgh at the time. Neither of us went to Carnegie Mellon University. We weren't building a life sciences company or a medical device. I was young, and Josh was even younger. Neither of us were engineers. We were just a couple of very optimistic, creative, stubborn people who had a great idea and a whole lot of drive and passion.

Our company didn't fit the mold either. Nobody in Pittsburgh was investing in web-based software companies. We knew that we'd never get anyone to write us a check unless we were able to share actual results with them. We needed to show growth, traction. Any line we showed potential investors needed to point up and to the right.

Having started an internet company, we knew investors would be looking at two particular metrics closely: traffic and users. "Engagement" wasn't as much of a thing yet. The big question we faced: how could we drive traffic to the site *and* get visitors to create accounts? We needed to prove to any potential investors that we could do it. We started to brainstorm.

Who were we hoping would create accounts? Since the first version of ShowClix was a live music search engine, we decided to target young people in big cities. This is where most concerts were taking place.

Next question: where were those people online? They were messaging each other in AOL chat rooms, hanging out on Myspace, looking for apartments and used furniture on Craigslist, and reading celebrity gossip on Perez Hilton's site.

In 2006, pop culture, fueled by the internet, was enjoying a moment of insanity. Paparazzi were swarming celebrities to get exclusive photos. Facebook opened its virtual doors—to *everyone*. Dick Cheney shot a guy in the face. Jack Dorsey sent the first tweet. Justin Timberlake brought "Sexy Back." Britney Spears began her downfall. And in the center of it all sat Perez Hilton. He broke major Hollywood news stories by posting photos of celebrities with doodles on top of them on his blog. An extremely popular blog.

Would Perez do something with us? How could we get his attention? What carrot could we dangle in front of him to make helping us worth his time? We were a brand-new startup with no name recognition, no web traffic, and no users. We had to get creative. Luckily, this was one of our favorite things to do. We loved nothing more than brainstorming ideas all the way to absurdity and then backing off just a little to the point of crazy but possible.

We knew several important things. One was that Perez Hilton *loved* two British artists more than nearly everyone else in the world: Amy Winehouse and Lily Allen. Their recently released albums were blowing up the charts and were stuck on repeat in the Spreadshirt office. We also knew that Amy Winehouse was in the middle of an extensive North American tour. Our idea: put together a promotion for Perez Hilton that gave away a pair of tickets to every Amy Winehouse show in North America. We were convinced his readers would love it. All we needed to do now was convince *him* that his readers would love it. We had to pitch him.

Josh was a master internet sleuth. It took him less than thirty minutes to track down Perez Hilton's personal email address. We drafted a message explaining our idea and, fingers crossed, hit send. Perez responded way faster than we were expecting him to. He was totally into it!

During the next several hours, Josh built a landing page that would be hosted on our website. Perez Hilton readers would be directed to our landing page to register to win Amy Winehouse tickets. We'd manage that part of the promotion, and every registration would create a new ShowClix account. The promotion would run for a couple of weeks. The traffic would inflate our numbers, and our new user registrations would climb along with it. If this promotion worked, we might just gain the traction we needed to talk to investors.

Did I mention that we didn't actually have any Amy Winehouse tickets yet? While Josh was building the landing page, I scoured the internet, scooping up tickets to all her shows in the United States and Canada.

When the promotion went live, the traffic hit hard. The landing page crashed, but we recovered. We did more than recover. We drove hundreds of thousands of page views and more than sixty thousand new user registrations. Vanity metrics, yes, but that was what mattered at the time. We fucking nailed it, and all it took was $500 worth of concert tickets and a whole lot of sweat equity.

Josh and I worked well together from the very beginning. He made me laugh harder than anyone else could, possessed the same sort of drive and passion I had, and wasn't afraid to take a whole bunch of risks with me. Perhaps his biggest was coming out to his blue-collar and devoutly Christian parents, a process I went through with him. In turn, he was there for me when Ryan and I got divorced.

Josh and I were there for each other during some of the most pivotal moments of our lives, and I expected it would be that way forever. We were going to build an incredible tech company and be best friends forever.

That was the dream anyway.

CHAPTER FOUR

Planting the Early Seeds

MARK SEREMET RAN United States operations for Spread-shirt. He's the main reason Spreadshirt decided to open an office in Pittsburgh. Mark has quite a résumé. He created the Grand Theft Auto video game series. One day Mark turned to me and said, "You're going to be a millionaire by the age of thirty-five. I just know it." There's something about having someone who's been successful telling you they believe in you. Sometimes that's all the spark you need.

Mark was also an angel investor and one of the few people in Pittsburgh writing about startups and tech. He had a blog that people actually read. When we launched ShowClix, I asked Mark to write about us, and he kindly agreed. The post couldn't have been more than two hundred fifty words, but that's all it took.

After reading Mark's blog post, Corilyn Shropshire, a tech reporter for the *Pittsburgh Post-Gazette*, wrote a short paragraph about the launch. Alan Veeck, a partner at Meakem Becker Venture

Capital, Pittsburgh's biggest VC fund at the time, read that paragraph and reached out to schedule a meeting with us.

I had no idea what to expect. I'd never met a venture capitalist before, let alone pitched one. That said, we'd been preparing for "this meeting," or one just like it, for the past six months. We'd finished the business plan, and the new version of the website was live. The all-important line on the chart was pointing up and to the right. We entered the meeting full of confidence and caffeine and ready to pitch. We left with nothing more than a reality check. They had no money for us. In fact, Meakem Becker never had any intention of investing in us when they reached out. Thankfully, they were upfront about the real purpose of the meeting once we got there.

Alan had reached out to us because Meakem Becker was working to create a startup scene in Pittsburgh, and he wanted to get to know some of the city's young entrepreneurs. Alan was helping to bring Open Coffee Club to Pittsburgh. A real-world meetup where entrepreneurs, developers, designers, and investors could chat and network in an informal, unstructured setting, Open Coffee Club had become popular in cities worldwide, and now it was coming to my hometown.

I was excited that Alan had thought to include us. I appreciated the feedback he gave us on our pitch deck and the advice on raising money. And I was thrilled when he gave us a referral at the end of the meeting.

"You know who you should talk to?" Alan said. "Jim Jen at Innovation Works."

Innovation Works was, and still is, the most active seed stage investor in Pittsburgh. Given where we were in the process, this was *exactly* who we needed to talk to. Alan made the intro later that day, and Jim responded quickly. After we exchanged pleasantries over email, he invited us in for a meeting in a couple of weeks. Josh and I allowed ourselves a few fist pumps and high kicks before we got back to work.

Meeting day arrived. We were scheduled to be at the Innovation Works office in the afternoon. That morning, Alan happened to be hosting the second Open Coffee Club in Shadyside, an affluent, tree-lined neighborhood in Pittsburgh's East End. I figured I'd swing by, grab a cup of coffee, and say hello before picking Josh up to go to Innovation Works.

The crowd for Open Coffee Club at the Coffee Tree Roasters on Walnut Street was small. There were maybe ten people there when I arrived—all white guys in ties. This was the norm in Pittsburgh at the time, and while I'd grown used to this dynamic, it was still intimidating and extremely frustrating. Where were the entrepreneurs who looked like me?

I grabbed a coffee and sat down in the circle. While introducing myself, I discovered I was sitting next to Bob, one of Jim Jen's colleagues at Innovation Works. *What a coincidence,* I thought. Small world.

"No way!" I said. "I'm heading to your office this afternoon to meet with Jim Jen."

"Oh yeah?" Bob said. "What are you meeting about?"

I gave him the quick version of the ShowClix pitch.

"Oh, we'll never invest in that," he said matter-of-factly.

What the fuck? That was *not* what I wanted to hear from anyone. That it came from someone who actually worked at Innovation Works made it doubly painful. In an instant I went from being incredibly optimistic about a potential path forward for ShowClix to being completely deflated.

While the man was an asshole, he wasn't lying. You see, what I didn't know then but do now, is that up to that point in its history, Innovation Works had been investing almost exclusively in life sciences, robotics, and advanced materials. Pittsburgh was (and still is) heavily grounded in "eds and meds."

As I walked to my car, I called Josh and told him the story. "Should we cancel the meeting?" I asked.

We agreed that it was likely going to be an awful meeting, but we had to do it anyway.

After picking Josh up, I drove to Innovation Works' office on Technology Drive on the South Side. To get to Jim, we had to push a whole bunch of buttons on a phone in the empty lobby. I was a mix of excitement and nerves that skewed heavily toward the latter. I was definitely sweating.

Jim was a smart, likable, and quirky guy. He asked great questions about our growth and tried to poke holes in our revenue plan. He walked us through the ins and outs of Innovation Works, gave us some great advice, and was amazingly patient. Most importantly, I could tell he cared about us. He had a genuine interest in discovering where Josh and I came from, what was driving us, and what sort of vision we had for the future. That day, Jim Jen became our champion. He ended the meeting by telling us that he wanted to introduce us to the rest of the gang and that he'd set it up.

After a few more meetings, pitch decks, and spreadsheet reviews, Innovation Works lifted the velvet rope. We were invited into due diligence, the part of the process where the investor makes sure that they're getting what they were sold in the pitch. Due diligence always takes a while, so we put our heads down and got back to work, hoping to plant some more seeds.

A big part of getting a company off the ground is refining the story that surrounds it. I'm a storyteller at heart, so I love this part of the process. As Josh and I refined our vision of the company, our story started to emerge. It was almost too easy. We were the underdog. We were David, and everyone knew who our Goliath was: Ticketmaster.

In 2007, Ticketmaster dominated the ticketing industry. It was the unquestioned leader in that space, a title it had held for the thirty-one years it had been in business. Upset about the steep service fees Ticketmaster charged, Pearl Jam tried to make a stand in 1994. The group was one of the biggest rock bands in the world at the time, but its attempt to change Ticketmaster's business model backfired. Ticketmaster was the '90s version of the tech giants—Apple, Google, and Facebook—that exist today. No one loves a monopoly, but they sure are hard to break up.

To differentiate ourselves from Ticketmaster, we planted our flag squarely in innovation. We wanted to build tools that would change the event industry. On our first attempt, we launched as an all-mobile ticketing company. We were finding our place in the market, which at that point wasn't super crowded.

As we morphed from an idea into an actual business, it became clear that we needed a supporting cast, particularly an attorney and an accountant to ensure that we weren't doing anything dumb or illegal. Unfortunately, we didn't take the time to find the right people. We went the convenient (and cheap) route instead. My Uncle Nick kindly offered to pay to have his attorney handle the paperwork pertaining to the company's formation, and who could say no to that? His attorney was fantastic but not somebody we could afford long term.

When we created the LLC, bylaws, and operating agreement, we solidified our titles. Since Josh had come up with the initial idea, he'd be CEO, and I'd be president. Who cared about the titles anyway? Especially at this point. I certainly didn't.

For the accountant, we chose the most convenient path once again, hiring a guy who worked directly upstairs from our office. *Big* mistake. He did the accounting for a bunch of small businesses in Oakmont, the leafy suburb where I grew up, but he knew nothing about tech companies. We had a few disagreements, to say the least.

> Advice: paying more to get the right attorney
> and the right accountant is worth it, even at
> this early stage. Don't be afraid to approach
> the biggest and most prestigious firms. Some

> of them are willing to offer startup rates, rolling
> the dice right along with the founders. If your
> company survives and thrives, the firms will
> get their standard rates down the road, and
> they'll be able to bill even more hours as your
> operations grow more complex.

How was I supposed to know that, though? I was navigating blind. I didn't have a real mentor at this point. Being a founder is never easy, but it can be especially difficult for a woman in tech. It's hard to be what you can't see. I had lots of advisors early on—the people at Innovation Works were particularly helpful—but I hadn't found someone I could truly confide in. Someone who wouldn't judge me for the way I *felt* while starting a company. I was always surrounded by men when what I really needed was another woman to give me support and guidance.

I'll admit I didn't try hard enough. I didn't understand how much I would've benefited from the right person's guidance.

Of course, the most crucial need at this stage was funding. That concern disappeared on a beautiful September afternoon in 2007. I was standing in the middle of Market Square, surrounded by an alarming number of pigeons, when my phone rang.

It was Jim Jen. "Good news, Lynsie! I just got out of the board meeting. Innovation Works is going to invest."

My smile threatened to tear my face in two. I couldn't believe it. We'd just landed our first funding! And it had all started with a single blog post.

Josh and I had known for a while that ShowClix wasn't a side project. It had grown to the point where we couldn't limit ourselves to working on it only in the evenings or on weekends. The only way we were going to be able to take it to the next level was to go all in. Our next move involved very little thought or discussion. We headed straight back to Spreadshirt's office and quit our jobs—effective immediately. We couldn't wait to start focusing on our startup full time.

In hindsight we got lucky early on. We never had to pitch hard for this first round of funding. Our timing lined up with a shift in the entrepreneurial ecosystem in Pittsburgh. The investors in the city were looking for people like us and companies like ours. Web-based companies. Software as a service (SaaS) businesses. They'd been watching the trend on both coasts for years, and these were the companies that were growing the fastest, so they finally decided to join the party, and there we were with just the sort of company they were looking for.

Our relationship with Innovation Works was a partnership from the beginning. They helped us. We helped them. Isn't that how it's supposed to work? They gave us $150,000 in seed funding, which they distributed to us as we met certain milestones. They liked to spoon-feed first-time founders their funding.

I took a $30,000 pay cut to make this work. I'd finally gotten to the point in my career where I wasn't constantly broke, only to agree to an arrangement that would all but guarantee I'd be broke for at least another five years.

Josh and I set a budget and goals that would stretch that money as far as possible. We thought we could make it last six months. We made it last nine. During those nine months, we found our first clients and exactly what we'd been hoping for—actual demand for our product.

Now we just needed to capture it.

CHAPTER FIVE

Learning *All* the Jobs

A FTER RAISING OUR seed funding, Josh and I leased a small office in Oakmont. It was one big room with a few make-shift walls thrown up to create separation. Before we moved in, my dad and I painted it a deep navy blue and gray to match our brand colors. Two big glass windows at the front of the office over-looked a convenience store that had a very popular payphone. Yes, a working payphone that accepted quarters for calls. From my desk, I frequently imagined the sordid subjects being discussed on that phone: love affairs, drug deals, even bank heists.

Having our own physical space seemed like an important step. It made our web-based company real. Josh and I set up our desks on the left side of the office. We were separated by a wall with a hole in it that looked like a giant drive-through window. We spent a lot of our days yelling things at each other through that hole: ran-dom questions, lunch ideas, song requests. But most of the time, we used it to transfer calls back and forth between us.

Whenever the phone rang, whoever was closest would pick

it up. It didn't matter who or what the caller was asking for. We would always transfer the call to the other person. We thought that would help us look more like an actual company.

For example: "Hi. Thanks for calling ShowClix. This is Lynsie. How can I help you? Okay, one sec. Let me transfer you to Josh, our director of sales."

I'd then press hold and yell through the hole, "It's some guy named Bruce from a blues festival in Wisconsin. You're the director of sales."

Next call: "Hey, Lynsie. I'm transferring a woman named Monica to you. You're in charge of marketing."

Next: "Hey, Josh. Paul wants to talk to someone in accounting."

In the entertainment industry, perception is *everything*. If people knew that ShowClix was just two people in a one-room office in Oakmont, they'd never choose to work with us. We had to make our operation look bigger and more established than it actually was.

That's how our days went, with Josh and I transferring calls back and forth to each other, pitching our software and answering questions. We'd take breaks for ping-pong and beers (as is required in any tech startup), but otherwise we were laser-focused on hitting the milestones Innovation Works had set for us. To do that, we had to do *all* the jobs: the ones we liked, the ones we didn't like, even the ones we didn't really know how to do.

After raising money from Innovation Works, I spent a lot of time with two people: Jim Jen, our executive-in-residence, and Frank Demmler, a longtime startup investor and advisor. The two of them had helped countless founders find success. We were overjoyed to have them on our team.

As Josh and I walked them through our plan to hit the milestones, we brought up the first hire we wanted to make. We wanted someone on our team who specialized in sales.

"Don't do it," Jim said. "Nobody knows your product like you do. Nobody cares about your product like you do. Nobody is going to sell it better than you." To this day, this is still some of the best advice I've ever received.

So obviously, I didn't listen. One week later, we hired someone to sell our product for us. It was one of the worst decisions we made.

There were others. When Josh and I started ShowClix, we set out to build a solution from the ticket buyer's perspective. At our core, that was who we were: a couple of pop culture fans who wanted to improve the ticket-buying experience. Our goal was to lower service fees, deliver tickets faster, and provide exceptional customer support. But our mission contained a major flaw: we weren't selling our software to ticket buyers but to venues and event promoters, and they didn't give two shits about the ticket buyers, service fees, and customer support.

What we didn't know until we tried to sell our software is that we weren't building the right product. We knew the *entertainment* industry well, but we had a very limited idea of how the *ticketing* industry actually worked. We knew that Ticketmaster dominated the industry, but we didn't fully understand how it did it. Venues and promoters don't pay Ticketmaster for its software. Nope. To protect its top position in the market, Ticketmaster pays venues to sign an exclusive agreement with the company. These "signing bonuses" range in size from $10,000 to more than $250,000. I know a music promoter who bought his house with a Ticketmaster signing bonus. That's how big these bonuses are. After Ticketmaster has the rights to sell tickets for a particular venue locked in, it jacks the service fees on the tickets and makes customers cover the additional cost.

This business model was bad for music fans and worse for any companies looking to enter the market and compete. I've always believed that you have to be a little naive to take the leap as a founder. If you knew exactly what you were getting yourself into, you might not do it. But our ignorance about what we were up against in daring to take on Ticketmaster slowed our ability to grow ShowClix early on.

Our optimism and naivete led to other problems. We were determined to take an entirely different approach to the business and launch an all-digital ticketing company—a radical idea in 2007. This led to an immediate problem with all the ticket scanners on the market at that time. They were created to scan barcodes. We were building software that would deliver tickets as QR codes. Luckily, we found a solution when we partnered with an Australian company called bCODE.

Shortly afterward, we landed our first in-person pitch. We were so excited to finally show off our new, innovative ticketing solution. On a crisp autumn afternoon, Josh and I walked into the Pittsburgh Improv carrying one of bCODE's massive ticket scanners, which neither of us had built or knew how to use very well, and it showed. We spent the first ten minutes of the meeting trying to get the scanner to work. Not the best way to start a demo.

It got worse. After we finally got going, we spent the next thirty minutes pitching the general manager and marketing director a solution they didn't need. Honestly, we had no idea what these people needed. I walked out of the building and through the parking lot knowing there was no chance in hell we were winning the deal. We were asking them to change too much about their business and giving them too little in return.

That we'd hired someone to sell this "solution" was almost laughable. There was no way my longtime friend Dave English, who we'd hired to lead sales, was going to be successful. Sure, we'd given him some good talking points and a loose sales process, but what we hadn't given him was much more important: a product the market actually needed.

The next time Josh and I met with Jim, I told him the sales guy we hired hadn't worked out.

He could have said, "I told you so." Instead, he got us back on track. "Looks like it's time for *you* to sell."

As soon as we started selling, everything changed. Almost overnight, things started to click. And I discovered that we'd been putting the cart before the horse. Instead of building something and trying to sell it, these initial sales calls helped us figure out what we needed to build.

First, we realized that the ticketing software wasn't really the problem. The problems were things like:

- Current solutions were old, and they weren't flexible enough. Venues and event promoters couldn't try new things, even if they wanted to.
- Venues and promoters didn't have access to their customer data. Ticketmaster wouldn't hand that over.
- While larger venues and promoters got bonuses for signing multiyear deals, Ticketmaster did the opposite to smaller venues and event promoters: it charged them setup fees.

The current system was fucked, and we only figured out exactly how fucked it was by *selling our own product*. It wasn't until we got on the phone, asked probing questions, and listened to people's stories that we started to build something that the market needed. The best way to know what customers want is by talking to them—period. The tidbits and gems I learned during these phone calls helped me build a better business—a business that focused on real problems plaguing real people.

As a founder, I'm always learning. I knew nothing about digital marketing, user acquisition, or lead generation when I started at Spreadshirt. Once I got in there and saw what we needed to do, I taught myself how to do it. I'm still learning all the time. It's a required skill in the tech startup world, where the landscape is constantly changing.

The flipside to this is taking on too much responsibility. In Show-Clix's early days, I was responsible for all things accounting, legal, and HR. I had no business doing any of this, and I absolutely hated it.

The accounting work included paying our clients every week. This was a key differentiator for us early on. To minimize risks such as cancellations, our competitors like eTix, Tickets.com, and Brown Paper Tickets didn't pay their clients until after the events they'd ticketed had taken place. This hurt small event organizers who needed the money upfront to ensure that the event would actually take place. Weekly payouts were an essential component of our business model—for our clients and for us.

Every Tuesday, I locked myself in a conference room with Rob Powers, the amazingly upbeat engineer we'd recently hired, and we calculated how much we owed each of our clients. I plugged the amounts into a third-party payment platform and sent them on their way. Then I plugged the same amounts into the ShowClix database so our clients could see how much money was coming their way. The process was labor-intensive and prone to human error. There was so much room to make a mistake, and it constantly stressed me out. Every Tuesday sucked. When people came to the office that day, they knew better than to approach me. These days became known as "Don't Talk to Lynsie Tuesdays."

I made some miscalculations along the way. I reversed numbers, missed client payments, and sent one client's money to another client for several weeks. Asking for cash back is never fun. Mistakes like these lead to hard conversations. People *really* don't like it when you fuck with their money.

I learned to do the dirty work without complaint. I stuffed envelopes and ran them to the post office when we had to pivot from all digital to more traditional ticketing. I took hours and hours of customer support calls. I apologized to angry clients. I didn't do these things because I wanted to. Context switching all day every day is extremely challenging. And I didn't do these things because I hoped it would pay off down the road. I did them because given our limited funding and lack of personnel, I didn't have a choice.

Josh and I did every job until we couldn't do them anymore. We were smart about it. We couldn't afford to increase our burn rate, so we didn't throw people at problems. Instead, we rolled up our sleeves and did the work ourselves. We made a lot of mistakes and suffered a lot, but we also learned a ton along the way, and our company became better for it.

Josh and I were good at shuffling responsibilities. We had complementary skillsets with just the right amount of overlap. If a department or project needed special attention, one of us would shift our focus to the task at hand while the other picked up the slack on the other side of the office. It worked really well.

There was a certain beauty in embracing the pain of every job. Because I'd developed all the initial processes, later on down the road I was able to empathize with team members and provide advice based on firsthand experience. Interviewing new hires also became much more manageable since I knew exactly what it took to get each job done.

With most of the things I needed to learn, I dove in headfirst. I watched every tutorial and read every how-to guide. There was lots of trial and error in the beginning. That didn't bother or scare me. But for some reason, selling did.

Why didn't I want to sell? Why was I so excited to hire someone else to do this job? It's not like I hadn't already done a ton of selling to get to this point in my life. I just hadn't called it that. When I was making lattes at Starbucks, I was selling people more than their caffeine fix. Why else would they spend five bucks for a cup of coffee? As a music publicist, I'd paid my dues banging phones and sending cold emails. How was that different from what I was expected to do now?

I'm an extroverted introvert, which means I do well socially as long as I'm given an opportunity to recharge my internal battery in between engagements. Selling forced me to break out of my protective shell. It also forced me to listen to very honest, raw feedback about the product we built. It's hard to listen to negative feedback about a business into which you've put all of your energy and focus, and it really sucks to hear the word "no" over and over and over again.

All the negative responses made me feel discouraged, embarrassed, and sad. I was beaten down and exhausted after working the phones all day. But the flip side made it worth it. When the calls went well, I learned exactly what our market wanted. I got real-time product feedback, which in the tech startup world is gold.

Once you get over your initial fear, selling can be a lot of fun. You get to insert your personality into the business. When I write emails, they sound like me, not some advertising copy. I like researching clients and customers before I talk to them so I can get a sense of who they are. I love reading Wikipedia articles about prospects' hometowns before I call them. If I find something unique or interesting, I ask them about it. It's an easy way to start a conversation. People love to talk about themselves! Then I pitch the product and work my way to a yes or no as fast as possible. That's the goal. It's simple.

There was no downside to selling. None. I learned a ton about our customers, the market, and our competition. I identified opportunities I never would've known existed. I found new channels for customer acquisition. And I learned which questions to ask in order to get the response I was looking for, the all-important yes or no. Side note: I ended up being pretty good at sales.

Now that we'd figured out how to sell our product and generate revenue, it was time to add some people to the team.

CHAPTER SIX

Hiring the First Crew

MATT DONNELLY HAD just graduated with a music business degree from Northeastern University in Boston and was anxious to start his career back home in Pittsburgh. His interview went really well; in fact, he seemed like the perfect fit. I liked him immediately and was excited to offer him his first job.

I consider myself a good judge of character, but I was forced to question my judgment the following Monday when Matt walked through the door on his first day with a scraped face and a broken tooth that had "bad night out" written all over it. *Welp, I guess we'll see how this goes.*

Surprisingly, it couldn't have gone better. Matt was smart and fast, and he got shit done. He was also willing to do whatever it took to make our clients happy. During his time at ShowClix, Matt helped close some of our biggest deals and did a dizzying number of jobs, earning promotion after promotion. He was one of the best team members you could ever ask for.

Hiring people is scary. Especially the first few people. It feels so "make or break," and for us it really was. After two years of struggling to get our heads above water, we needed help. There was so much work to do. We couldn't do it alone. If ShowClix was going to match the vision we had for it, we needed intelligent, capable problem-solvers on our team.

There's additional pressure when you're making the first few hires because these people will set the tone for your company. They'll create its culture. From the very beginning we had a great culture at ShowClix. We truly liked each other, had fun every day, and wanted to be successful together. Did I get lucky? Maybe, but I also had a process for hiring that worked really well for me.

People often ask me, "What did you look for in the first people you hired at ShowClix?"

What founders look for in early team members is very personal and unique, but I'll tell you what mattered to me. When someone joined ShowClix in 2009, they spent a good part of their first day assembling their own desk chair. Josh and I didn't have the time or expertise to put together a bunch of desk chairs for people. More importantly, having to perform this task gave people a good idea of what life was like at ShowClix. We needed people who could do this—whatever "this" was.

Would this new hire survive the zombie apocalypse? Because that's what a startup feels like. At times you're just trying to *survive*. Not everyone is built to work at a startup. Some people *think* they want to work at a startup but realize they've made a horrible mistake once they start working there. There's no process, no HR, no toilet paper. It's not pretty, people!

I had a series of questions I asked myself when interviewing potential team members:

Will the person sitting in front of me love or hate startup life? In other words, does this person enjoy a structured, process-driven environment, or do they thrive in organized chaos?

At a startup, everyone does everything. Startup people are asked to do things they'd never have to do at a corporate job. They are asked to do things that aren't in their job description (gasp!). No job is beneath anybody. Find people who understand that and are more interested in being part of a team and supporting the mission than caring about the bullet points on the job posting.

Will they take chances, be curious, learn quickly, and be unafraid to break things along the way?

I hired a lot of people who'd just finished college. What they didn't have in experience they made up for in curiosity and a willingness to learn whatever it took to get the job done. If an answer wasn't apparent, these people sought it out.

Will they see their role as a job or as an opportunity to build a career?

The original ShowClix crew grew with the company. They started out doing all the jobs, and they found their specialties along the way. In the beginning, we had two account executives: Matt Donnelly and another one of our first hires, Erin Borger, whose responsibilities included:

- responding to inbound leads
- demoing the product
- closing deals
- providing ongoing support to the clients they closed

When the inbound leads started pouring in and our client list began to grow, it became clear that we needed to divide this role into two different jobs: sales (the person who closes the deal) and client services (the person who supports the client after the deal is closed). Josh and I talked to Matt and Erin and explained the change we wanted to make. Erin chose sales, and Matt went with client services. They grew their careers in these specialties, but only after learning how to do a bunch of other jobs first.

This sort of thing happened all the time in the beginning. We'd hire someone to fill a role, and that role would morph into something else based on that person's strengths. Whenever we created a new position, we always tried to hire from within before advertising the job to the public. A decade later, seven of our original ten team members were still working at a much larger version of ShowClix, and all of them were in leadership roles.

Will they look for ways to help beyond their standard "job responsibilities"?

Our brilliant CTO Nate Good did this all the time. Hiring—and retaining—engineers got way more complicated in 2011, after Google significantly expanded its presence in Pittsburgh. As soon as Google's fancy new office doors opened, it started recruiting every good startup engineer in the city. Its recruiters offered big salaries and Silicon Valley office perks. The average Pittsburgh startup couldn't compete.

To stave off the enemy, Nate came up with a fun recruiting idea. Once a quarter, he invited engineers from all over the city to our office. They ate shitty pizza, drank local craft beer, and sparred in roundtable discussions on practical (and occasionally weird) engineering topics. He called it "Engibeering." After registering to attend the event through ShowClix, engineers received one of our mobile tickets. The barcode that the engineers used to get into the event also activated the office kegerator. Scan the barcode, get a beer. It was so nerdy and so fun. Engineers loved it. Our team loved it. I loved it.

Not only did this quarterly event help Nate recruit great engineers; it also kept the existing crew happy. They were able to meet other people in the tech scene and talk about current topics of interest. Even our nontechnical team stuck around for Engibeering. Not because they had to but because they wanted to. They liked learning from the engineers (and drinking the free beer). After Nate launched Engibeering, we never had a hard time hiring engineers, because engineers were eager to work with the guy who'd come up with an idea like that.

Side note: Nate Good had *a lot* of good ideas. He's one of the best things that ever happened to ShowClix. And we found him through a Craigslist ad when he was twenty years old.

Do they care about the mission?

Ticketing live events should be easier for everyone involved. Smaller independent venues shouldn't get fucked over by Ticketmaster. People organizing small one-time events should have an easy way to sell tickets and bring people together to have a good time. And people going to events shouldn't be pissed from the outset because they had to pay a service fee equal to 20 percent of the ticket price.

Artists and creators were drawn to ShowClix. From the beginning our office was filled with creatives, including musicians, DJs, producers, dancers, actors, and writers. One guy, Ted Zellers, frequently competed in unicycle races—and won! These people understood and were passionate about the event industry. They'd felt the pain as organizers, performers, and fans. They were drawn to ShowClix because it allowed them to be a part of an industry they loved and work with people they related to in some way.

Our nontechnical team came from amazingly diverse liberal arts and humanities backgrounds: journalism, sociology, English, and history. They brought so much to the table, including unique, people-first skills that helped solve a lot of problems.

For years, *Consumerist*, a now-defunct consumer affairs publication, ran an annual "Worst Company in America" contest. A series of reader polls determined the winner. The contest had a tournament format similar to college basketball's March Madness. Ticketmaster was one of the top three most hated companies in America *three years in a row* (2009, 2010, and 2011). Fans deserved better. We wanted to give them great tech, fair prices, and incredible customer support. We believed that to the core. It was an integral part of our mission.

We didn't just preach our mission; we lived it. Our customer care lines were buzzing on a summer day in 2010 when a call came in from an older woman who was having difficulty printing the tickets she'd purchased from us. She didn't have a smartphone, so she needed to print the tickets to get into the event. After a few failed attempts to help her, the team summoned Ryan Hurst, our director of customer care.

Ryan had an immense amount of patience and a genuine interest in helping others. He happily hopped on the phone with the woman. After several more failed attempts to help her print the tickets, he noticed the event was taking place in Pittsburgh.

"Where do you live?" he asked her.

"Shadyside," she said.

"Let me just print these for you here, and I'll drop them off on my way home from work."

When he showed up at the woman's house, she

greeted him at the front door—in a nightgown. Thanking him repeatedly, she even insisted on giving him a tip.

That's how much our team cared about our clients and customers. They'd literally go the extra mile for them.

How are their writing skills?

I'm a journalism major and a lover of language, so this is a big one for me. I don't care what the position is; I'm always looking to hire a person who has excellent writing skills. Good communication is key to the success of any startup. You're moving fast, and everyone has to be on the same page. A lot of the communication is written. We're constantly pecking away at a keyboard, shooting off Slack messages, creating bug tickets, and drafting emails. And the written communication isn't just internal. We're constantly communicating with clients, customers, and partners as well.

Great writers will have an impact on every aspect of your business. Their proposals will close more deals. Their emails will create happier customers. They'll provide your engineering team with clear product feedback. So hire great writers.

Do I like them as a person?

We spend *a lot* of time with our work families. Sometimes more than we do with our actual families. I've developed some of the most amazing relationships and friendships through work. I've also been forced to spend an inordinate amount of time with a few people I didn't care for very much. For me, one of the biggest benefits of being a founder is that I get to pick the core team. I get to decide who I spend my time with every day. We work long hours and often travel to events together. I'd better like these people.

Nathaniel Minto joined the team as project manager in 2010. He was more buttoned-up than the rest of us and wasn't interested in mixing his personal and professional lives. He showed up at the office every day in a well-coordinated J. Crew ensemble, sat down at his desk, and got to work. No small talk. No dilly-dallying.

His reticence and obvious intelligence intrigued me. I wanted to get to know him better, because as the project manager, he'd be interacting with every department. He was going to be a key member of the team. I frequently poked at him, asking him questions and suggesting we go to lunch together. Nothing. He wasn't budging. Making him my friend became my mission. When I found out we lived just a few blocks from each other, I started offering him a ride home after work so he didn't have to take the bus. Then I'd take the longest route home I could think of, peppering him with questions about his family, friends, and dog the whole way. He caught on to my scheme, but I eventually cracked him, successfully forcing him to be my friend.

Trust is important to me—always has been—and I needed to know if I could trust Nathaniel to be one of the people who helped make the hard decisions. In the process, he became one of my closest confidantes. To this day he still helps me make a lot of my most challenging decisions, and he's one of my best friends.

"This is one of the reasons we're such good friends," he once said to me.

"Why?" I asked him. "Because I'm really funny?"

"No. Because you're incapable of lying."

Multiple people have told me that I'm "brutally honest." In a male-dominated environment like the tech startup world, this trait is often viewed negatively. I'm honest to the point of bluntness, and men don't seem to like it when women act like that. They always take it the wrong way. More than one man has called me "aggressive." They've taken a positive characteristic and turned it into a negative one. Being a woman in tech, even the tone you use is often misconstrued.

Surrounding myself with the right people was one of the best things I did at ShowClix. We developed some great working relationships that allowed us to be honest with each other because we all trusted each other. Think hard about what you're looking for in your early team members. Keep in mind that these will be the people sitting at the table with you when you're thinking through and making some very difficult decisions. Hire smart people. They will challenge you and make you a better person. And make sure the team is well rounded and diverse. You need to hear different opinions and perspectives on every issue.

Once you've assembled your supergroup, it's time to close some deals and make shit happen!

CHAPTER SEVEN

Landing the Pivotal Deals

Tens of thousands of people were swirling around me, their faces obscured by masks. I slowly started to recognize them. Harley Quinn. Chewbacca. Loki. Kahn. Was that a nine-foot-tall Iron Man Hulkbuster? You bet it was.

Welcome to New York Comic Con.

As cool as it was to attend the event and witness all this pop culture goodness, it paled in comparison to the fact that ReedPop, the event's organizer, had just agreed to let us ticket the event the following year. That was pure magic.

ShowClix didn't get there overnight. Not even close. In fact, for a brief stretch in the company's history, we got an astonishing percentage of our revenue from ticketing male revues. That's right, male strip shows. Our internal slogan during that period was "ShowClix: we'll ticket anything!" Needless to say, this is not what we *wanted* to be doing.

When we created ShowClix, Josh and I had hoped to work with small, independent, live music venues. When doing my initial research, I reached out to a couple of music promoters in Pittsburgh and asked if we could meet. I didn't intend to pitch ShowClix. The solution hadn't been built at this point. I was looking for feedback, which they provided at a very high level. If I would've been paying more attention, I would've recognized their complete lack of interest. These guys weren't interested in the tech. The tech they were using wasn't great, but it worked well enough.

The music industry simply didn't care about what we were attempting to do. It was the worst possible fit for us. We were committed to technology and innovation, and they didn't give a fuck about technology and innovation. They were much more interested in maintaining their deals with Ticketmaster and raking in as much cash as they possibly could.

We needed to find clients who were looking for an alternative to this outdated business model, who weren't afraid of change, and who wanted to build better relationships with customers and fans. Unfortunately, we weren't in a position to hire a sales team, and Josh and I didn't have the time to go out and find the clients— at least that was the bullshit we told ourselves.

Instead, we brought the clients to us. We were still riding a steady wave of inbound leads from our Google search ads. They were all over the map, but every once in a while, a gem would land in our laps. In the summer of 2010, two great opportunities came our way, either of which would have had a major impact on our business.

After hearing about us through some work we'd done with *Billboard* magazine, the folks at the Museum of Modern Art (MoMA) in New York City reached out. They were launching a unique film series, and the system they used for daily admissions wasn't a good fit. They needed a timed ticketing solution that would also support their memberships.

As a bit of an art nerd, I was beyond excited about this opportunity. I knew that MoMA's name would open doors for us at museums around the country, if not the world. The association would elevate our brand at least ten levels above ticketing Chippendales events. This deal could change things. The only problem? We hadn't built timed ticketing yet.

That same week, we got a call from Doug Meckler. Doug was the founder of an eco-conscious ticketing company in Australia called Greentix. He was working with some of Australia's biggest festivals and needed a new ticketing partner *fast*. He needed a private-label solution that was customized to his exact specifications. Nobody out there had built exactly what he was looking for. We definitely didn't have what he needed. Not even close.

After talking with MoMA and Doug, five of us sat around a conference room table, talking through everything we'd have to do to secure and execute one of these deals. Everyone on the team would have to pitch in if we were going to pull it off. We decided to divide and conquer. I took MoMA.

By this point I loved working the big deals. I enjoyed getting to know the people on the other side of the table. I looked forward to asking tons of questions. I found pleasure in learning about their business. There was always something beneath the surface that was driving them, and their challenges were always unique.

Within two weeks, we signed both deals. And the following six months? Fucking insane.

Damn. This better work.

Nate and his engineering team pulled off an unparalleled feat. They built the functionality needed for MoMA's film series by deadline, an impressive feat on its own, and at the very same time they built a private-label ticketing platform that could sell tickets in any currency or language. I don't know exactly how they did it, but they did, and I will forever be in awe of this accomplishment.

The MoMA launch was smooth. Doug's launch? Not so much. Did I mention that Doug was a wild man? While working with clients, you get to know them pretty well. We definitely got to know Doug. While we were building his private-label platform, we were in constant communication with him—on the phone, over instant messenger, and occasionally in person at our office. He'd roll in from San Francisco, reeking of weed, and immediately fire up some reggae music. He talked fast and barely listened.

Doug was crazy, but he also made shit happen. He ticketed lots of festivals that hosted anywhere from ten thousand to fifty thousand fans throughout a weekend.

The first Greentix event to go on sale through ShowClix was Equitana. The horse event, of course. This isn't just any horse event, though. This one attracts more than fifty thousand people every year. Unfortunately, these horse fanatics experienced a few glitches during the on-sale. It wasn't a total disaster, but it was far from perfect. That said, at the end of our first day on sale in Australia, we'd sold $1.8 million worth of tickets.

The future was looking bright! Our segments were starting to bubble up to the top. We were beginning to figure out what sort of events made sense for us to ticket. We'd learned that certain types of event organizers were a much better fit for us than others.

The people who were seeking us out weren't interested in the signing bonuses offered by Ticketmaster and its younger rivals, TicketWeb and Ticketfly. Their focus was finding a ticketing solution that solved actual business problems and worked well for customers. They were innovative. They wanted to work with a company that was building new shit, not just keeping old shit from toppling over. Our focus on innovation was starting to pay off.

We charged ahead, building new features, onboarding bigger clients, and supporting more and more fans. The stakes kept getting higher. The more prominent and high profile our clients were, the more important it was to get shit right. We were overwhelmed, overworked, and stressed out. But we were happy. Shit was starting to come together.

A few months later, I was sitting in my living room on a Saturday night, looking for something to watch on Netflix, when I came across *Indie Game: The Movie*. This documentary shines a spotlight on the video game industry's underdogs, the developers who sacrifice money, health, and sanity to share their video games with the world. It's a look inside the life of a different kind of entrepreneur, the tortured video game artist.

The documentary is filled with footage of PAX Prime in Seattle. Originally known as the "Penny Arcade Expo," PAX is a series of gaming festivals involving tabletop, arcade, and video gaming. It's one of the largest video game expos in the world. This is where independent game developers come to unveil their creations to more than sixty thousand video game fanatics who are eagerly waiting to get their hands on the latest, greatest games.

My mouth dropped as the camera panned the long line of people waiting to enter the event to be part of the experience. They'd swarmed the internet to get tickets. I turned and looked at my boyfriend David and said, "I wanna ticket that."

I'm a big believer in serendipity. I had beseeched the universe, and the universe was listening.

Two weeks later, an inbound lead came in from Randy Field, vice president of operations technology at Reed Exhibitions. I wasn't familiar with Reed, so I consulted Google, which told me Reed Exhibitions was an event organizer with a portfolio of five hundred events in forty countries, including the UK, Austria, the US, France, Germany, Brazil, Russia, India, China, Australia, and South Africa, as well as several countries in the Middle East. I couldn't pick up the phone fast enough to give him a call.

As it turned out, Randy hadn't reached out to us to talk about working with Reed Exhibitions. Bummer. He wanted to talk to us about working with Reed Exhibition's quirky offshoot, ReedPop. Fuck yeah!

ReedPop is the largest producer of pop culture events in the world, including New York Comic Con, the Chicago Comic and Entertainment Expo, Walker Stalker Con, and PAX. At that moment I was absolutely positive that I'd willed this connection into existence, but Randy insisted that he'd actually found us through a Google search ad I was running.

A few weeks later, Erin, Nathaniel, and I headed to ReedPop's office in Connecticut. This was ShowClix's A-team. There was no chance we weren't getting this deal. We were ushered into a conference room lined with posters of all the amazing events these people had painstakingly brought into existence. People from ReedPop started to file into the room.

Lance Fensterman, the mastermind behind ReedPop, sauntered in last. Wild hair, cool glasses, jeans, and Chuck Taylors. He was around my age and had an "aging hipster" vibe about him. He said fuck within minutes of meeting us. He said fuck a lot. I loved him immediately.

Lance told us stories about ReedPop's history and evolution. We talked about high-demand on-sales, RFID admissions, cashless payment, and fan engagement. Lance was hyper-focused on innovation and doing what was best for the fans. I left that meeting convinced that ReedPop was going to give us a shot, and I was right.

The risks we'd taken with MoMA and Greentix were starting to pay off. The tech we'd built for these clients put us in the perfect position to take on one of the biggest challenges in ticketing just a year later: New York Comic Con.

My life wouldn't be the same if Randy and Lance hadn't believed in us and given us a chance. Over a decade later, ReedPop is still ShowClix's most active and innovative partner. I'd finally gotten to the place I wanted to be, working with people like Lance and Randy on events like PAX and New York Comic Con.

These pivotal deals brought with them many ups and downs. Managing relationships with big clients is hard. You want to push the limits for them—build cool shit, make their lives easier, make them more money—but with greater expectations comes greater pressure. One big client can have a very real impact on your revenue. If you fuck up, it doesn't just impact them, but you and your business as well.

Navigating and structuring major deals can be challenging. Don't fall into the trap of allowing them to be one-sided in the client's favor. Don't promise customization at no additional cost. Some clients will try to suck up development resources in a way that's detrimental to the rest of your customer base, your engineering team, and your company. Learn to say no early on or find a way to satisfy the client that makes sense for you too.

Attracting more big clients involves a virtuous feedback loop. To continue to land big deals, you have to execute on the big deals you already have. You need your high-profile clients to be willing to act as references for you, to be interviewed for case studies, to let you use their logo in your marketing, and to help you grow faster if you manage them the right way.

You need to learn how to navigate the tricky balance between how much to build for them and how much to build for everyone else. The best-case scenario is the partner who pays for the development of features that everyone will use, but that doesn't happen often. If a client asks you to do custom work that won't benefit other clients, you should pause and ask yourself whether it's worth doing. First, ask some of your other clients if they might be interested in using the new feature. Better yet, ask them if it's something they might be willing to pay to use.

ReedPop was smart. It structured the relationship with ShowClix in a way that forced us to crawl together before we ran together. The first few events we did with ReedPop weren't its largest, most high-profile events. ReedPop's leaders weren't dumb. They knew shit could (and probably would) go wrong, and they didn't want to risk having an epic fuckup during one of their high-profile on-sales.

We were smart too. We never assumed we knew more than they did—even when it came to the ticketing technology. We learned from them, and eventually we learned *with* them and collaborated with them. We were only able to do this because they were the perfect partner for us. They thought like us, and they operated like us. They truly cared about their customers. They didn't just want to create events; they wanted to create *experiences*. That's why we—ReedPop and ShowClix—do what we do.

Landing these big deals pointed us in the right direction. MoMA and ReedPop drove other museums and pop culture conventions our way through referrals and exposure at their events. The day we signed the deal with ReedPop was one of the high points of my time at ShowClix. We were now ticketing some of the biggest, most high-profile pop culture conventions not just in the country but *in the world*. Our scrappy little startup team in Pittsburgh had built something that was truly amazing.

CHAPTER EIGHT

Surviving the Epic Fuckups

I HAVE FOND MEMORIES of our first real fuckup at ShowClix.

Steel City Big Pour, an annual fundraiser for the nonprofit Construction Junction, is one of the most popular craft beer events in Pittsburgh. Historically, its online ticketing had been a disaster. Demand was always extremely high. Events and ticketing weren't part of their team's daily schedule, so it was simply too much for them to handle. Before reaching out to us in 2010, they'd experienced major complications two years in a row.

By this point, ShowClix had ticketed quite a few big events, many of which were much larger than the three thousand tickets we had to sell for Steel City Big Pour. The morning of the on-sale, we walked into the office full of confidence, ready to kick ass and save the day for a high-profile event that a bunch of our friends and family attended every year.

The tickets went on sale at 10:00 a.m., and almost immediately, our website crashed. It didn't go down for just a little bit. Nope, it was *down* down. All. Damn. Day.

As soon as people realized they couldn't buy tickets online, they flooded our phone lines. We were instantly overwhelmed. And then the worst possible scenario occurred: since the event was local, the organizers decided to roll into our office to talk, unannounced, in the middle of the chaos.

What they walked into only existed because we'd hired the right people and built a team that believed in the mission. Every single person in the company was on the phone talking to disgruntled beer lovers. The founders, the COO, finance, sales, marketing, support, engineering. *Everyone* chipped in. Okay, most of the engineers were sweating profusely while trying to fix the problem, but those who were available were fielding customer calls.

We wrote down the name of every customer who called, their phone number, which session they wanted to attend, and the number of tickets they wanted to purchase. When the engineers finally put all the pieces back together, the same people who had been answering the phones all day stayed at the office late to return every single call in the order they'd been received until the tickets were sold out. It was the longest day ever, but we made sure that every person who wanted to buy a ticket to Steel City Big Pour was able to do it. At the end of that day, I knew without a doubt that we could and would survive anything together.

Five months later, we sent our team to Steel City Big Pour to work as admissions volunteers. Armed with new scanners, we admitted ticket holders into the event in record time: seventeen minutes. Our commitment to the event and our willingness to do the dirty work must have impressed the organizers. Ten years later, ShowClix is still ticketing the event.

Bad shit is going to happen. How you manage it is what matters. What clients and customers need most in moments like this is honesty and transparency. Never lie to them. Don't make promises you can't keep. And never compromise your integrity. Once you've lost someone's trust, it's hard, if not impossible, to win back.

We didn't do enough of this in the beginning. We were so focused on signing deals and generating revenue that we'd make promises we couldn't keep. We'd shoehorn events into our system that had no business being there. Whenever we did this, the event organizers and ticket buyers were never happy. Guess who else wasn't pleased. Our team.

In some ways, our self-confidence was understandable. Our engineers were amazing. Our client services team was thorough and exacting. Our customer support team was filled with warriors. Given all this talent, we never wanted to believe we couldn't do something.

By this point the Museum of Modern Art in New York City had an equally lofty view of our capabilities. We'd been working with them for more than a year, and they'd been happy with the functionality we built for their film series and had seen us successfully manage several high-demand on-sales. So when they were planning a unique experience that involved a high-profile music residency, they thought of us first. I was pumped. I saw a lot of opportunity in the market and knew that expanding our relationship with MoMA could help us gain ground. Have I mentioned that I *loved* working with MoMA?

We got on the phone with the team at MoMA, and they walked us through the details. The museum would be hosting a series called *Kraftwerk – Retrospective 1 2 3 4 5 6 7 8*. Over eight consecutive nights, MoMA would be presenting a chronological exploration of the iconic German band Kraftwerk. Each evening would consist of a live performance and 3D visualization of one of Kraftwerk's eight albums in the order of their release. The band would follow each evening's performance with additional songs from their catalog. The event was going to feature Kraftwerk's complete repertoire, an unheard-of undertaking for most bands, particularly one of Kraftwerk's stature.

If you've been living under a rock for the past fifty years, Kraftwerk is one of the most revered bands in the world. They are widely considered to be the innovators and pioneers of electronic music and were among the first to popularize the genre. In short, the announcement of this residency was going to blow their fans' minds.

Of course, there was a catch—and it was this catch that would be one of our biggest challenges. Of the thousands of tickets available for the eight-night run, only a couple hundred per night were going to be sold to the public, and the people at MoMA were estimating that more than one hundred thousand people would be hitting the site trying to get those precious few tickets.

This was a nightmare scenario. When they pitched the idea to us, part of me knew that we shouldn't take it on, but, fuck, it was MoMA, and it was Kraftwerk! We had to try, right? Adding to the intrigue and level of difficulty, MoMA explicitly stated that we weren't to talk about how many tickets were available to the public. Nobody was to know that the actual chance of getting a ticket was about 0.05 percent.

After the call, we sat down as a team to discuss it. Nate and the rest of the engineering team embraced the challenge and were eager to take it on, which swayed the rest of us. *All right then. Let's do this!* We spent the next few weeks building the event in the system. Testing. Tweaking. More testing. Finally, everything looked good. *This better work.*

The day of the on-sale arrived. February 22, 2012. A day that will live in infamy—at least at the ShowClix office. We huddled together and very impatiently watched the minutes tick down to the noon on-sale time. That's when the floodgates opened. Fast and hard. More than 150,000 people were on the website *instantly,* and just as swiftly the site crashed. My heart sank. I watched as the engineering team scrambled to figure out what was causing the issue. Our phones blew up. Irate Kraftwerk fans bombarded our customer support team with calls.

Fuck. I knew I had to call MoMA ASAP. I hated this part.

I headed across the office toward Josh's desk hoping to talk to him about the call to MoMA I was about to make. Josh had been checked out for a while now—I'll be discussing the story behind that in just a bit—but it wasn't until this moment that I learned just how checked out he really was. While everybody was running around, fielding calls and doing their part to save the company, he was casually walking across the office to the front door.

He stopped me before I could launch into the frantic speech I'd prepared. "I'll be right back. Heading out to get a haircut."

Wait, what? He was getting a haircut *now*? Well, okay, then.

As he walked out the door, I was shocked, but I was more concerned about the MoMA call. I grabbed the key members of our internal MoMA team and headed for the conference room. I felt like I'd been kicked in the gut as I dialed the phone and waited for someone at MoMA to pick up. I had no idea what the ramifications of this mistake were going to be, but they couldn't be good. I *really* didn't want to lose this client. I started apologizing, and explaining what had gone wrong on our side, before whoever had picked up the phone could say anything.

Monica at MoMA cut me off. "It's fine! Don't worry about it."

Wait, what? Everyone at MoMA was incredibly, and shockingly, understanding. They understood the unique nature of this event. They understood the unprecedented stress that they were putting on our system—so much demand for so few tickets. They actually kinda loved the way things turned out. The Kraftwerk tickets were so coveted, demand for them had crashed the internet! They weren't mad at us. They weren't going to sue us or do something insane. We weren't even going to lose their future business. Big sigh of relief. Phew.

The media wasn't so forgiving. Here are a few of the headlines that appeared online—and all over Twitter—in the wake of the fuckup:

"Computer Hate: No One Got Kraftwerk Tickets"—Vice

"Most Kraftwerk Fans Scheisse Outta Luck"—Gothamist

"Kraftwerk At MoMA #TicketFail"—HuffPost

"ShowClix CEO Responds to Kraftwerk Nightmare"—Inc.

Nightmare. That was the perfect description. Thanks, *Inc.* You guys nailed it.

Next up on the apology list: Kraftwerk fans.

Fans were always the most challenging part of the business. Not because they flooded the phones and social media with complaints and accusations. Not because they were so hard to please. And not because their expectations were so high. Because they were us and we were them. Accommodating their desire for a simpler, cheaper, and more efficient way of getting tickets to see their favorite artists was the main reason we started this company. We wanted to make the ticketing industry fair and easy for everyone, not a nightmare.

The next day, Josh and I conferred with our team and drafted a letter that explained to Kraftwerk fans why they were unable to get tickets to any of the MoMA shows. We put ourselves in their shoes and tried to be as honest and transparent as possible. We wanted them to understand that we felt their pain and understood their frustration and anger.

The letter we crafted and posted on our site explained, perhaps in too much detail, the technical glitch that occurred. A single setting within one of the lower levels of our queuing system's middleware bubbled up under the heavy load and caused frequent timeouts. We didn't properly prepare our load-balancing servers to prevent the queue from timing out. There were also some issues with the broadcast system that allowed us to communicate with ticket buyers while they were waiting in the queue.

Did knowing *exactly* what occurred completely alleviate Kraftwerk's fans' distress? Probably not, but it was important for us to clarify what happened as a way of addressing the (false) reports swirling around the internet that our servers had crashed or gone offline.

The trickiest part of writing the letter was explaining the true cause of the problem—the technical hurdle created by having so much demand versus so little supply—while at the same time respecting MoMA's wishes that we not disclose the limited number of tickets that were available for these performances and the fact that even if everything had gone right, very few Kraftwerk fans would have been be able to buy tickets.

The most important parts of the letter, paraphrased here, required the fewest words:

> *We are deeply sorry. We let you down. This is no excuse. We take full responsibility.*

Could we have done anything better? Obviously. When we first sat down with MoMA to discuss the event, there was concern around the numbers from the beginning. Selling hundreds of tickets to hundreds of thousands of people on demand is complicated—and it really doesn't make very much sense.

After hearing the details of the event, we could have pitched a solution that wasn't the new, shiny cloud-based queuing system we'd developed. We could've suggested a lottery system, which was much more common at the time. We should've been more honest and transparent with MoMA about our concerns. We failed to do that because we didn't want them to think we weren't capable of doing the job. We'd presented ourselves as being the innovative, underdog ticketing company. We loved pushing the limits. There was no task we couldn't handle. But in this instance our ambition and risk tolerance backfired on us.

We definitely should have had a better backup plan. If we'd spent more time talking through worst-case scenarios beforehand, maybe our reaction to the screwup would've been faster, and we might have gotten better results.

The fuckups never end in the startup world. Some of them are big, and some of them are small. The one constant is that people are watching. How you respond to each crisis either helps your company continue to grow or hastens its demise.

While a lot of stuff went horribly wrong on that February day, our fast and honest response to the mistake earned a ton of positive press, which ended up outweighing all the criticism we'd received. We didn't lose clients; we actually signed new clients. And we formed new relationships with people, organizations, and events that wanted to work with an innovative company that wasn't afraid to take risks.

So don't be afraid. But do be prepared.

CHAPTER NINE

Picking the (Wrong) Investors

RAISING MONEY IS hard. It sucks. I hated it. You might be one of the rare entrepreneurs who loves building projections and pitching old white guys. If so, raising money might be a little easier for you. For the rest of us, though, it's the hardest and most painful thing we have to do.

I wasn't and never will be very good at asking for money. With the exception of one uncle, I didn't come from a family that had a lot of money. When I was a kid, my parents told me it wasn't appropriate to talk about money. Now I'm supposed to ask strangers for money?

The process seemed like a charade. At the end of every pitch, I wanted to look across the table and say, "We all know this is bullshit, right? The projections, the roadmap, the plan. We don't know what the fuck is going to happen over the next sixty days, let alone the next five years."

I did it only because I had to. We'd stretched the 2007 seed funding from Innovation Works as far as we could. We made the first $150,000 they gave us last nine months. We made it to breakeven. We made the next $150,000 they gave us last two years. We ran super lean from the very beginning. We had seven people on the team now, but we were still pulling off insane startup moves. It wasn't sustainable, and it wasn't scalable. We needed funding.

By 2009, we were sitting in the middle of a highly competitive industry filled with extremely well-funded competitors. If we were going to keep up, let alone survive, we needed additional funding ASAP. We'd been operating with a skeleton crew. We needed more engineers. We needed a sales team. We needed people to help support our growing list of clients and their customers.

While we were confronting this new reality, our seed investor, Innovation Works, launched a competition that would award one new investment fund in Pittsburgh $1 million. Innovation Works hoped this fund would fill the gap between seed investments and the growth-stage funding the region so desperately needed.

During an event at Carnegie Mellon University in 2009, I ran into Jonathan, the managing director of New Pittsburgh VC Fund, the fund that received the $1 million "prize." We agreed that we should talk. The dance started: pitch decks, projections, legal reviews. I'd met Jonathan a few times over the years. He was friendly. He seemed harmless. He was tied to Innovation Works, so I was happy to talk to him.

But this tie to Innovation Works ended up being a curse. Josh and I became victims of circumstance. Because Innovation Works had provided some of the money to start Jonathan's fund, there was a conflict of interest. The people at Innovation Works, the people who had been our biggest mentors, weren't able to advise us on the round. They weren't allowed to be part of the discussions. They couldn't review the term sheet with us.

We didn't have an attorney we trusted at this point. Jonathan wanted to help us fill this void, so he introduced us to a local attorney, and we hired him. We were so naive, so trusting. Of course, we shouldn't have hired an attorney who was closely connected to the fund we were negotiating with! Ah, hindsight.

A couple of months later, in August of 2009, ShowClix became New Pittsburgh VC Fund's first investment. They were the lead investor in our $1.3 million series A round. My excitement was tempered by a reality check down the road once I was more educated on fundraising. There's no way in hell this should've been called a series A, but that's what they called it. They demanded and got series A terms for only $1 million. The terms we ended up with were equivalent to what a VC investing $10 million would have gotten. We gave up too much equity too early. It was a huge mistake, but we didn't know any better, and it really wasn't a problem—until suddenly it was.

After closing the round, we immediately added a few people to the team. We needed to release some pressure, move faster, and plan for growth. This was the first time we'd had a cushion, runway, actual money in the bank. We could finally attract (and afford) someone with real experience to help us drive the bus. That guy was Tom Costa.

Jonathan introduced us to Tom, who showed up to his "interview" wearing a really cool leather motorcycle jacket. Did Tom ride a motorcycle? No, he was just that awesome. Tom was *by far* the best thing that came out of our series A round.

I was in desperate need of a COO. I couldn't manage the finance, HR, *and* operations work while running sales, marketing, client services, and customer care. It was too much work for a single person to handle, and that work was getting more and more complicated. We got flooded with résumés after we posted the job. So. Many. Résumés. Most of the applicants were way too corporate. We needed someone with startup experience. Somebody who wasn't going to be afraid of the chaos. Somebody who would help us transform that chaos into process. We needed somebody who would be patient with us and teach us but continue to let us take risks and be creative.

Tom was perfect. Prior to joining ShowClix, he'd started and sold four companies. He was a pro. With him in the office, I finally felt like I had someone who could provide guidance and support. He was an ear for me to vent into, a wise, experienced operator, and he was happy to share all that he'd learned. He didn't want to be the face of a company anymore. He didn't want to be CEO. He wanted to help a young team that was eager to grow and be successful. He wanted to keep us focused and headed in the right direction. And he wanted to keep our heads out of the clouds and our feet on the ground. He was so good at reining in our crazy ideas that we started calling him the "Dream Crusher." It was absolutely a term of endearment.

One of the first things he did after coming on board was find us a new attorney, a guy who actually knew what the fuck he was doing. The deals kept rolling in. Revenue was growing, and life was fucking good.

Actually, it was better than good. It was great for two years until, out of the blue in late 2010, Rich Lunak, president and CEO of Innovation Works, sent us an email introducing us to Clive, the managing director of Corporate Guy VC Fund.

"Clive just moved to Pittsburgh from London," Rich explained, "and is getting a fund off the ground. He's interested in talking to you about investing in ShowClix."

Rich had been a huge supporter of ShowClix from the very beginning. He was a good guy. I trusted him. We weren't currently raising money and didn't need the money, but we wanted to keep the good times rolling and thought it wouldn't hurt to bring in more capital, so we scheduled a meeting.

We met Clive for the first time shortly after moving into our new office in Shadyside, our third office in three years. As good as we were at ticketing cool pop culture events, we were equally bad at picking office space.

Whenever I meet someone, I'm all about the vibes, and right off the bat I wasn't digging Clive's vibe. He had a smug face, eyes you couldn't trust, and one eyebrow that always pointed slightly up. The former CEO of T-Mobile UK, Clive came from a corporate background and had never worked at a startup. He'd never even worked in software. But what *really* bothered me was that during that entire ninety-minute meeting, he never asked me a single question or even addressed me directly. He did make sure to mention that he was friends with a guy who worked with Dave Matthews—like that might impress a bunch of people who'd worked in the music industry.

My wish in these situations was always the same. I just wanted the person sitting across the table from me to look or act or think like me, but I never got that. What I got was a smug, buttoned-up suit like Clive.

The next thing I knew, we were in due diligence. Clive wanted to invest. Innovation Works would participate again. Same with Jonathan and two new angel investors. With Tom sitting next to me, I felt so much better this time around.

Unfortunately, our backs were already against the wall. The terms we'd agreed to with the series A round were coming back to haunt us. We'd given up too much equity too early. For this round, I wasn't as worried about the terms as I was about a question lingering in the back of my mind: *is this the right person to join our team right now?* Fuck. This was so hard. How are you ever supposed to know if it's the right investor, the right amount, the right time?

One thing I've learned is that *every* venture capitalist promises three things when they invest in your company:

1. Money (obviously)

2. Guidance, mentorship, advice

3. Introductions

All startups desperately need these three things, but all we ever got from our series A and series B investors was money. Based on conversations I've had with founder friends who aren't in Silicon Valley, I believe this is common. These investors love to overpromise and underdeliver.

I remember feeling uncomfortably anxious while standing in a dark corner of a packed restaurant in New York City. I was on the phone with Josh, talking about the term sheet we were getting ready to sign. The place was so loud I had a hard time hearing everything he was saying, which amped my anxiety since we were talking through a major decision. Among the many problems I had with Clive investing was that accepting his money meant he would be chairman of the board. He'd be in charge. My gut, my head, everything inside of me was screaming, *Don't do it! Don't take this guy's money!*

In the end Josh and Tom convinced me that if anyone could help us get to an exit it would be a guy like Clive. They sold me, and I bought it.

One of my biggest regrets was not evaluating our investors the same way I had my co-founder and every early team member. I should've spent more time considering this one fundamental question: *do I like this person as a human being?* For some reason, I minimized the importance of this question once we started meeting with investors. I thought I didn't have much choice. If someone was offering me money, I was going to take it. I didn't know there were other options.

I also didn't realize how serious a company's relationship with its investors is. You won't spend as much time with your investors as you will with your co-founder and team members, but you will still spend a lot of time with them, and during this time you'll make some pretty important decisions together. Ideally, you should like these people. You should definitely respect them. At the very least you should trust them. Life will be much easier if you do.

We accepted $1.65 million of series B funding in March of 2011, and it ruined everything. I should've trusted my gut. Even though Clive had invested the least amount of money in the series B round, the fact that he'd led the round made him chairman of the board. He was now in charge, and he made it clear from the outset that he'd be running the company his way from now on. He immediately introduced a level of formality to ShowClix that was more typical of a large corporation than an early-stage startup.

Clive often said that he "knew what was best" for our startup company—even though he had no idea what actually went on in a startup. Making the message feel even worse was the way it was delivered. He always spoke softer than everyone else in the room. You really had to pay attention to what he was saying just to hear him. It was a fucking power move, and you can't convince me otherwise.

Over the next few years, with Clive at the helm, our investors chose to spoon-feed us dollars instead of actually investing in us. They pushed for the leanest operating style possible, with the goal of reaching breakeven. I appreciate this approach to growing a business—when it makes sense—but at this point we'd more than proven our product-market fit. It was time for us to make a move, damn it!

Alas, these guys were never going to let that happen. They sacrificed the growth of the company in order to maintain control. We limped along. The vibe in the office started to change. Worse, my relationship with Josh started to change.

Before he'd even invested, Clive started driving a wedge between me and Josh. Prior to closing, Clive *never once* had a one-on-one meeting with me. In fact, he never had a one-on-one meeting with me for the entire five years we "worked together." He only met with Josh because Josh was the CEO. I guess titles *did* matter, at least to Clive. Josh's CEO title overshadowed the partnership the two of us had formed years before. Didn't Clive realize that Josh and I had built this company together from scratch? He didn't seem to care about that, and he started to force Josh into a role that I don't think Josh ever wanted to play. Josh responded by pulling back from the company a bit. Suddenly, he seemed interested in everything but ShowClix.

Shortly after raising the series B, we pushed hard to hire someone with industry experience. It had become clear to me that the ticketing business was very much a relationship business. It was all about who you knew and who they knew. We didn't know *anybody*. We needed someone who thoroughly knew the space to hop on board and drive our outbound sales and partnership efforts. Doug recommended a guy from the Bay Area named Jack. According to Doug, Jack had *tons* of industry experience.

Perfect. Jack knew lots of people in the industry and had previously worked with one of our biggest clients. He understood exactly what Doug needed, and he could help manage the relationship. We flew him in for an interview.

Jack was nice, but I couldn't tell if he was legit or totally full of shit—and I consider myself a good judge of character. Once again, I didn't trust my gut. We brought Jack on board, and it was a total disaster. It quickly became apparent that he wasn't going to work out. For someone at the VP level, he required way too much hand-holding. I also didn't have the patience for his personality. He was the kind of guy who'd call you to "ask a question," and forty-five minutes later he'd still be talking—about absolutely nothing relevant. Being extremely task-oriented and impatient, I found this was a hard relationship for me to manage.

I was overseeing sales at the time and had been for the past year. Most of our leads were coming in through inbound marketing, so it made sense for me to take those from the top of the funnel to closed deal. My team had gotten really good at working that pipeline. The arrangement was perfectly fine until Jack's underperformance was brought up in our next board meeting. As I was explaining the hurdles I was facing managing Jack, Clive abruptly stopped the meeting and asked to speak to Josh in the hall.

After a few minutes, they walked back in and announced that I would no longer be overseeing sales. It was now Josh's department. They removed me from a position without even including me in the conversation, and I was a founder. Rather than working with me to fix the problem with Jack, Clive ripped a department out from under me without considering the impact it would have on me or the rest of the company.

That's when I knew just how different things would be. Clive had put a stake in the ground. ShowClix was no longer a company run by its founders. He didn't care about my opinion or my experience, and he never acknowledged or appreciated the results I'd generated, including signing our highest-revenue client to date.

In the beginning of Clive's tenure, I was still very much myself. During board meetings I led the sales and marketing presentation and helped brainstorm ideas. I also wasn't afraid to express my opinions in my trademark brutally honest style. Once I even had the audacity to disagree with Clive. We were in the office a few days later when the subject came up again. "Oh, great," Clive said, "this is what made Lynsie have a temper tantrum in the board meeting."

Temper tantrum? Would he have referred to it as a "temper tantrum" if Jonathan, Tom, or Josh had disagreed with him? I was so pissed. It was a shitty thing to say, and yet nobody else flinched. It was like I wasn't even there. I immediately called him out on it. I couldn't let that slide. How could I? I'd never been slapped in the face by gender bias until I worked with Clive, and then I experienced it more regularly than I could've ever imagined.

By the end of the first year, with Clive in charge, I felt horrible every day. I was tired. I was confused. I was emotionally drained. And I was depressed. I'm still on Paxil to this day.

> If you're ever faced with a choice between taking bad money or burning your startup to the ground, burn it down. I'm not kidding. Destroying something you've built sucks, but it will be fast, and it will be your choice. Taking bad money, on the other hand, will be something you have to live with every single day for as long as you both shall live. My entire life was turned upside down after we accepted the series B funding. I went from being a fun, caring, confident leader to someone who could barely get herself out of bed in the morning.

I felt broken. I was no longer comfortable in my own home. I once walked into the ShowClix office happy and confident, ready to tackle whatever problem our team faced that day. Now I doubted myself constantly. *What am I doing wrong? Should I be presenting myself another way? Do I need to tone down who I am to get my point across?*

As bad as it felt to be asking myself these questions, it felt even worse when I stopped. I didn't care about anything anymore. I stopped contributing during our meetings. Why speak up if you're not actually going to be heard? Why ask questions if you might get bullied?

My life was spinning out of control. Many of my personal relationships were falling apart, and my health was deteriorating. I felt completely alone. I was doing everything I could to hold on, but there were moments when I wasn't sure if it would be enough.

CHAPTER TEN

Losing a Co-Founder

THERE'S NO DOUBT in my mind Josh and I were supposed to meet. We were kindred spirits, both of us eternal optimists. Neither of us had any sense of direction—we once got lost in a mall together. We're both super Polish, and we loved that about each other. He made me laugh harder than anyone else ever had. Neither of us had any advantages growing up, but we loved pushing boundaries, and we hustled so damn hard.

It's difficult to write about everything falling apart, but that's what happened. Our relationship, as co-founders and as best friends, unraveled slowly. There was no single moment it all went south. No seismic shift. No stadium implosion. Huge life-altering changes like this often sneak up on you. If you're paying attention, you can see the signs, but if you're consumed by your job and your personal relationships (i.e., a normal person), you likely won't be paying attention. You simply have too many other things to deal with. And then one day, you wake up and everything is different.

Work wasn't as fun as it used to be. The vibe Clive brought to the office didn't sit well with anyone. He put a damper on our creativity. He demanded monthly board meetings, which meant we had to spend a lot of time—time better used elsewhere—prepping for board meetings.

Despite the no-fun zone we'd entered, the company was doing great. Thanks to our relationship with MoMA, an expansion into Australia, and a steady stream of inbound leads and referrals, we were continuing to grow at a rapid pace. And as usual, weird and exciting opportunities kept rolling in.

One day in 2013, we got a call from a much larger player in the ticketing industry, Cvent. The call came out of the blue, and the intent behind it was a little shocking. The company wanted to expand its presence down market. For the last decade it had been providing event management software to prominent corporate event planners and marketers. Its founder/CEO and senior leadership team planned to expand through an acquisition, and they wanted to see if we were interested.

Introductions were made over email. The CTO was from Pittsburgh. A Pittsburgh-based VC had invested in the company early. We knew some of the same people. That kind of stuff always makes the initial meeting easier. I love finding commonalities.

After we talked through the basics of our respective businesses over the phone, they invited us to visit their corporate office. Their interest in ShowClix was obviously real and strong.

Josh, Tom, and I hopped in the car and headed south. We spent the following day getting to know their team and swapping industry stories. Their founder shared his company's history, which was riddled with "Oh shit, this isn't going to work" moments that they'd managed to turn around in a very big way. I was impressed with everyone we met. At the end of a long, exhausting day, they made their intention clear. "We'd like to make an offer, and here it is." It was five times our current revenue—a solid offer.

We'd obviously talked about the possibility of this company making an offer, but we hadn't anticipated they'd do it so quickly. Taking into account the stage we were at, the competitive market, and the amount of money we'd raised, I considered it to be a fair offer, one well worth taking the time to mull over. From the discussions we'd had in the boardroom, I knew that Josh and I weren't totally on the same page, but I didn't know just how far off we were until this moment.

His reaction was unbelievable. He was *offended*, and he did nothing to hide his displeasure. He acted like a child, like a seven- or eight-year-old who wasn't getting his way. He was so disrespectful I was embarrassed.

His response wasn't entirely out of character. Up to that point in his life he'd never been told no. He was homeschooled by a mother who basically thought he was Jesus Christ, and then he went straight into the tech industry, and all his ideas had turned into gold.

The most frustrating part of Josh's response was that he never gave me or Tom or anyone else on our senior leadership team a chance to offer our input. He didn't even take a moment to think about it. We could have stepped outside and had a conversation. We could have waited to talk. Instead, Josh shut down the negotiation and burned the bridge that had connected us to this company. And all I could do was sit there and watch it happen.

At least I now knew exactly where he stood. He'd made it very clear.

We headed back to Pittsburgh the following day. The drive home was awful. I couldn't stop thinking about how far apart Josh and I were during that meeting and how far apart our desired outcomes for ShowClix were. In the beginning we both had grand visions for the company. As time passed, Josh's vision stayed grand. I became more of a realist. I began to see the writing on the wall. Josh still wanted the enormous, life-changing exit. I came to accept that this wasn't in the cards for ShowClix.

Our age difference and where we were at in our lives probably played a role. At this point, he was only twenty-four and still looking to conquer the world. I was thirty-four and had just found out that my boyfriend David and I were expecting. Most of my thoughts involved wondering what it would be like to run a tiny human startup. I knew my priorities would need to shift. Exiting at the number we'd been offered would've provided a lot of security for me and a baby, and working with this new company would've allowed me to learn from some exceptionally talented people.

Back in Pittsburgh, we convened the board and walked them through the meeting we'd had. Josh downplayed his interactions with Cvent's CEO. As we talked about the offer, the divide became clear. Josh and Clive were on one side of the table, Tom and I were on the other. Jonathan would be the tiebreaker, but there was no way in hell he was going against Clive, even if he needed the exit for his new fund just as much as I wanted it for the opportunity and security it would bring.

Josh and Clive were looking for an offer that had another zero at the end. I was bewildered by their delusion. None of us were on the same page. How the fuck was this going to work? It couldn't. We were forced to walk away from the exit.

A few weeks later, Cvent acquired one of our smaller competitors, Ticketmob. *Great,* I thought. *Another well-funded company we'll have to battle for deals.*

Josh and I were never the same after that. He continued to slowly back away from ShowClix. At one point he spent the better part of three months in Michigan filming a reality TV show called *Undercover Intern.* We barely saw him during that time. He never talked to any of us before agreeing to do this. He just disappeared.

The dynamic between us was awkward. I still loved him like a brother, yet I was so pissed at him for shifting his focus away from ShowClix, choosing to do something that was new and fun and bailing on me.

Just when I thought things couldn't get worse, I noticed some unusual activity while reviewing some of the company's credit card bills. A line item for a large purchase from the craft store Michael's caught my eye. Josh had apparently used one of the company credit cards to buy something for his new condo. It's incredible how much can change in an instant.

I started digging and discovered that he was spending money in ways I wasn't comfortable with. A payment to his interior designer. The purchase from Michael's. Lots of lunches and dinners with his significant other, who he hired after we agreed we would never do that. He didn't make these extravagant and unauthorized purchases every single day, but they occurred frequently enough that I was alarmed and annoyed. I could've looked the other way—until I realized that it was part of a larger pattern. My breaking point came when I found out that he'd advanced himself half of his yearly salary, paid out all at once, to buy his new condo. The only person he talked to about this was our VP of finance. I was left entirely out of the loop.

What? It was a significant amount of money to pull out of the company account at one time. A financial decision like this should only have been made after being approved by the board, but the board never even knew about it. Nobody did. There was so much semi-shady stuff happening under the radar—until suddenly it wasn't under the radar anymore.

I talked to Tom, and he told me that I had to tell Jonathan and Clive. He was right. I had no idea what to do in this situation. I needed advice. This wasn't something I ever thought I'd have to deal with. I called them separately.

Jonathan's response: "This is unacceptable."

Clive's response: "Let's talk about this."

We scheduled a meeting for the four of us to meet at Jonathan's office at the corner of Wilkins and Beechwood in Squirrel Hill. I still get sick to my stomach every time I bike past that building.

I went in expecting to be supported and hoping we could resolve this problem in a professional manner and move on. Instead, Jonathan and Clive hung me out to dry. As I struggled to talk to Josh about everything I'd found, they just sat there and said nothing. I'm not sure why I thought they would be helpful. They weren't. The hours I spent in that conference room with the three of them were without a doubt the worst I spent at ShowClix.

What made this situation even worse was that everyone, including me, would likely have been fine with the lunches and dinners and the salary advance *if Josh had bothered to ask us.* But he never did. He kept it from us like a dirty little secret. He lied, and that's an emotional trigger for me. I've always had trust issues, so when I realized that Josh had been lying to me, I was devastated. I'd never trusted anyone more in my life. We'd built an amazing company together. We'd experienced so many amazing things together. And he took a match and burned it all to the ground.

If he'd just come and talked to me about everything, we could have resolved this conflict and moved on because I was always on his side. Instead, he turned his back on me and moved on by himself.

The next two months were the most painful of my life. I went to work, but I was barely there. I had a corner office that was all windows, so I had no privacy, and I would just sit at my desk, practice French on Duolingo, and hope no one caught me crying.

At one point I only weighed ninety-five pounds, and I didn't drink alcohol for a year and a half because I felt like it was the only thing I could control.

Josh's lack of interest in ShowClix confused me until I discovered he was already chasing a shiny new object.

Following in the footsteps of Y Combinator (launched in 2005) and Techstars (2006), Innovation Works launched a tech accelerator called AlphaLab in Pittsburgh in 2008. The early version of ShowClix was exactly the type of company AlphaLab wanted, and Josh and I had worked with leadership at Innovation Works as they developed the program. They asked us questions, and we answered as best we could. We helped them figure out the kinds of things companies at the earliest stages needed to survive and thrive. We even helped them come up with AlphaLab's name—over a game of ping-pong, obviously.

Once AlphaLab was off the ground, Josh and I worked closely with some of the companies in the program. We hosted a session for each cohort and made ourselves available as mentors. Many of the founders I met through AlphaLab are still friends today.

A few months before I confronted Josh about the unapproved expenditures, he'd started mentoring a new AlphaLab company, Insurance Zebra. That's what I thought, anyway. Turns out, he'd been acting as much more than a mentor to this company, regularly working out of their office and managing large portions of their business. He'd joined this other company as a founding member and was helping them raise money. He had effectively quit ShowClix but hadn't bothered to tell anyone yet (or so I thought). And nobody seemed to give a fuck but me.

As soon as Josh's new company announced its series A funding, which included money from Mark Cuban, Josh officially resigned from ShowClix. That was it. Game over. He'd left me for someone else. And I finally figured out why Clive didn't give a fuck about Josh's self-serving behavior at ShowClix: he'd already invested in Josh's new company. How was that okay?

Everything was collapsing around me, and in the middle of all of it, I had a miscarriage and my relationship with my boyfriend of three years, David, fell apart. Without him I had no one to share my problems with. He had been my entire support system. There was no way I could confide in anyone on the team. That's one of the hardest and least discussed aspects of being a founder. You're all alone at the top.

After ShowClix grew to more than twenty people, Matt Donnelly pulled me aside one day. "Why don't you come out with us anymore?" he asked.

"I can't," I told him. "It was fine when it was just ten of us, but I can't be that person anymore. I'm supposed to be the leader of this company. I can't show that side of me now."

Only now do I realize what a huge mistake that was because hanging out with team members was always a big part of who I was. It was one of the reasons we were able to attract and build the amazing team that we did. We found people who actually wanted to be a part of the startup craziness, and it was beautiful.

So instead of hanging out with friends from work and getting the angst off my chest, I suffered in silence.

Tom was a great advisor and mentor, but at the end of the day, he was still a dude. He never fully understood how difficult it was for me to work with Jonathan and Clive. No one fully understood just how much I was falling apart, probably because the process was slow and occurring from the inside out.

When Josh resigned, Clive was eager to replace him with a new CEO from outside the company. I reluctantly agreed with the plan, but once again, I was much more realistic about the likelihood of this actually happening. They wanted to get someone with Silicon Valley experience and ticketing industry connections and couldn't see any reason that might not be possible.

What they didn't realize, because their egos were too big, was that from the outside there was nothing about ShowClix that was attractive to a West Coast leader. We were in Pittsburgh. We didn't have well-known investors or advisors. We'd only raised $5 million. We had no budget for hiring sales or marketing. We couldn't afford the type of person they wanted, even if that person existed. On top of all that, I was the only one in the room who knew anyone in the industry. I was the only one who'd gone to all the major conferences, events, and client meetings from the very beginning. Even though the CEO role was never in the cards for me, I couldn't believe they had the audacity to ask me to help them fill it with someone else.

After a piss-poor attempt at recruiting, we all agreed that Tom should be the new CEO. The investors liked him, and the team respected him. I was fine with this decision—until I realized how it would affect the rest of the board. Previously, Josh had the CEO seat, and I had the founder seat. Now Tom would have the CEO seat, and Clive and the rest of the board voted to give Josh the founder seat. I would have bupkis, nada, nothing.

Even after he'd been caught moonlighting, making questionable purchases on the company's dime, and advancing himself his salary without authorization, Josh retained his board seat. Yep, the founder who was leaving the company would still get a vote, while I was cast to the side. They'd finally succeeded in silencing me for good.

After Jonathan and Clive made Tom the new CEO, they decided that ShowClix needed to raise another round of funding. No shit. I'd been saying this for more than two years. In five years, we'd only raised $5 million. Meanwhile, Eventbrite and Ticketfly had raised $125 million and $75 million, respectively. Our good luck and charming personalities were only going to get us so far in this business.

At the next board meeting, Clive looked at me—directly this time!—and said, "Lynsie, your top priority right now is fundraising. You need to go out and raise another $5 million."

With Josh gone, it was all on me now. I was going to have to do the thing I hated the most—alone. Fuck. After a few days, I thought, *I can do this. I'll hate it, but I can do it.* After several more days, I began to see it as a lifeline. *No, I need to do this.* Raising a round of funding would change everything. It would mean a new group of investors, and a new group of investors would mean Clive would no longer be the chairman of the board and wouldn't have as much control over the company.

I had to do this.

Over the next six months, I traveled from one Rust Belt city to the next, meeting with investors and doing the thing I hated the most. I got a bunch of nos. But I also got two yeses. I put together a $6 million round with two venture capital firms, Draper Triangle in Pittsburgh and Mutual Capital in Cleveland. The term sheet looked good. After due diligence and legal, the VC firms signed the term sheet. I signed early as well because I was heading to the West Coast the following day. The board would be meeting two days later to take care of the rest.

I hopped on a plane and headed to Tahoe to meet up with my new boyfriend, Brian. He lived in San Francisco, and we'd been in a long-distance relationship for about six months. Did I mention he was senior vice president of sales for Ticketfly? Yes, I was sleeping with the enemy. Isn't that an essential part of any good story?

Two days after I signed the term sheet, I woke up to a call from Clive informing me that the board members had changed their minds. Clive wasn't going to sign the term sheet. We weren't taking the money.

What the actual fuck? It was hard to say whether I was more shocked, angry, or confused. I was definitely pissed that we weren't raising the round I'd worked so hard to get, but I was even more upset that they'd put my reputation on the line like that. I felt like such an asshole. I'd made commitments to people. Now they wanted me to call those people and say, "Just kidding! We're not looking to raise money anymore."

Why did they do it? I can only imagine that Jonathan and Clive decided they didn't want to give up control of the company because at the end of the day that was what they were most concerned about, control, and it was such bullshit.

Everything changed for me at that moment. My attitude experienced a seismic shift. I wasn't going to let Clive—or anyone else, for that matter—treat me like this anymore. I wasn't going to be silenced by fear. I wasn't going to let someone else control my happiness. If someone was going to destroy my happiness, it was going to be me, damn it!

I hung up the phone and turned to Brian. "That's it," I told him. "I'm done."

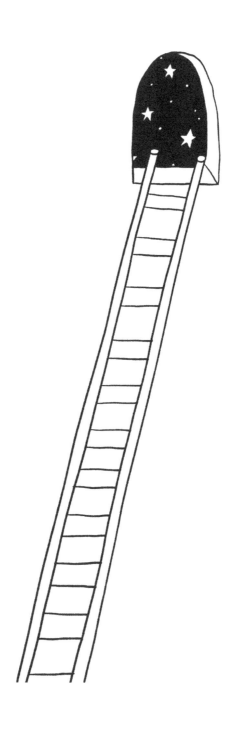

CHAPTER ELEVEN

Taking a Fucking Break

AFTER CLIVE REFUSED to sign the term sheet for the series C funding, I completely checked out. I couldn't bring myself to work hard for people who had no respect for me. Every meeting felt like a prison sentence. I'd become the burned-out startup founder you always hear about. The day-to-day grind, in addition to all the other bullshit I had to deal with, was exhausting. Working under those circumstances for the past four years had broken me. Clive and his corporate bullshit had broken me. I had nothing left to give. Some days I couldn't even decide what to eat for dinner. I was mentally and emotionally drained every single day. I felt inadequate in every possible way. I knew something needed to change, but I didn't know what.

A part of me wanted to burn everything to the ground, just to spite them. I didn't want to make these assholes a bunch of money they really didn't deserve. But I couldn't do it. The team was too good, and the people were too important to me. Plus the tech was so much better than everything else out there. I couldn't let myself burn it all down.

But I could leave.

I have a habit of running away from things when I just can't deal anymore. For me, the choice between fighting and fleeing is a no-brainer. I'm a total flight risk. I also like change. Combined, these two tendencies have put a lot of miles into my frequent flier accounts. I run from jobs, cities, friends, significant others, family. When I feel like I've tried to fix something, failed, and exhausted all my options, I bail. I know it's not healthy, and yes, I've talked to several therapists about it.

I needed to pull myself out of the ditch I was stuck in, so I came up with a plan. It wasn't a well-thought-out plan, but it was a plan nevertheless: I was going to move to San Francisco. It made sense. My boyfriend lived there. ShowClix was discussing mergers and acquisitions (M&A) with a few companies in the Bay Area. I could be helpful to ShowClix out West. I spoke to the people closest to me about my plan. Most of them understood. They could see, to some degree, what I was going through, and they wanted things to be better for me, for my mental health to improve. My family thought I was crazy, but they had no idea what was happening in my professional life.

"I'm moving to San Francisco," I told the board. "I'll work for ShowClix part time, focusing on partnerships and M&A conversations."

I felt like I'd earned the right to dictate the terms of my departure, so I didn't ask them; I told them. I drafted an email to the team with the investors CCed, explaining that I was moving to San Francisco, why I was deciding to take on a lesser role in the company, and what it meant for them. I was upfront and honest, just as I'd always been with this team. Without giving it a second thought, I hit send. It was now official.

I knew I'd made the right decision almost immediately. Right after I sent the email, Clive responded. He was upset that

I'd included personal details about the decision and thought I should've run my email past him first. Did Josh do that when he left? Hell, no. So fuck off.

Even though I'd thought through the ramifications of my decision, it was still a tough pill to swallow. I was no longer involved in the day-to-day operations of the company, and I wouldn't be overseeing my teams anymore. I still maintained a hope that I might be able to support those teams from afar. I could see myself jumping on sales calls with large prospects, visiting West Coast clients, and taking the M&A and partnership meetings in San Francisco.

None of that happened. As soon as I moved, I completely fell off ShowClix's radar—poof, gone, like a puff of smoke. Out of sight, out of mind. I think it was just easier for everyone to let me walk away, and nobody wanted to say that to my face.

I was heartbroken. My not-at-all-thought-out plan was not going as planned! I couldn't sit in a tiny apartment in North Beach by myself all day long, pretending I was actually doing something. I'm the type of person who always needs to be doing something. San Francisco was beautiful. I wanted to see more of it!

I asked myself, *What could I be doing that's not tech but that will get me out of the damn apartment and make me some extra money?*

Because I'm a relatively simple human being, my thought process probably went something like this: *Hmmm, what do I like to do? I like hanging out with my dog Peep. He likes to go for walks on the beach and visit cool places in the city. I'm sure other dogs would like to do this too. I'm qualified to walk dogs professionally, right?*

First was Apollo, a very spunky, apricot-colored miniature poodle. He was highly lovable, and he was my dog's BFF. Then there were Percy, Jackson, and Max. Then Dixie, Pico, Lily, Alfonso, and Daisy. I started out riding my bike from apartment to apartment, walking one dog at a time around the neighborhood where it lived. Soon I collected a bunch of them at once and walked them all together. "My minions!" I would yell, arms in the air, as I walked six of them across Crissy Field with the Golden Gate Bridge in the background. I was outside in the beautiful San Francisco weather hanging out with dogs all day long—what could be better? I'd get home after picking up eleven piles of dog shit, plop down on the couch, and smile. I was happy for the first time in a long time.

VITAL STATISTICS OF A DAY IN THE LIFE OF A DOG WALKER

- Dogs walked: 11
- Flights of stairs to walk-up apartments: 36
- Miles walked: 11.5
- Hours spent on beach: 2.5
- Dog shits picked up: 15
- Tennis balls lost: 1
- Tennis balls found: 2 (+1 on tennis balls—yay!)
- Puking incidents: 2

My typical workday was so lovely and so much fun that I decided to create a simple website. *Why not?* I thought. I put together a few price and schedule options, did some basic lead gen work, and promoted the business on Yelp and Thumbtack. I built an automated email campaign to follow up with inbound leads. I made it easy for people to get in touch with me, review a contract, and pay online. People in San Francisco really appreciated it.

The inbound leads came pouring in. The next thing I knew, I had more than thirty clients. Brian and I—okay, mostly Brian—bought a sweet van. I cruised around the streets of San Francisco, windows down, "Radio" from the new Sylvan Esso album turned up as loud as possible, a stupid grin on my face. The Marina. Cow Hollow. Pacific Heights. Russian Hill. North Beach. That was my loop.

Before I knew it, I'd started a dog-walking company. I called it Dogs Abide—a nod to *The Big Lebowski*. I used the tech tools many of my clients had helped build to drive them to my website to sell them dog walking services for $600 a month. There was something really satisfying about that.

Walking dogs helped me fix some of the things that were broken in my life. Even if it was "just a dog-walking business," the process of building something started to turn things around for me. It wasn't what I'd expected to do in San Francisco, but it was exactly what I needed to do to heal. Every day, I'd head out the door for two sets of walks: big dogs in the morning and small dogs in the afternoon. With my hands tangled in dog leashes, counting tennis balls, and shuffling apartment keys, I started to enjoy a different mindset and reconnect with myself on the streets, trails, and beaches of San Francisco.

There would be life after ShowClix after all.

There were many times throughout my founder journey when I had to start over, hit reset, and get my shit together. Taking a step back from business and life to do a full audit is never a bad thing. I do this at least once a year now. Life continues to evolve and change, so I embrace these resets as opportunities to look at the world with fresh eyes and assess what's important. Then I prioritize the things that bring me happiness and eliminate the things that don't.

When I started ShowClix, I didn't take a weeklong vacation for more than five years, which was a big mistake. What the fuck was I thinking? That would clearly lead to burnout. You need to completely unplug and explore a new place at least once a year, even if it's a new place right around the corner from you.

Part of the reason I took a break, and subconsciously why I turned that break into a business, was that I needed to prove to myself that I was smart and capable, that I could move on and do something else, that I could be successful, that I didn't need *them*.

The list of people I'd pushed under the umbrella of that term was long, but Josh was at the very top. Ever since I'd met him, he'd always been the golden boy, only eighteen and ready to take on the world, and I felt like people gave him a lot more credit for the work we did than they ever gave me. Running a close second were the investors who'd hurt my company and my personality far more than they'd helped. I didn't need any of them to be happy and successful and move forward with my life.

> If there's one thing I can't stand, it's people not taking me as seriously as they should. Part of this is my fault. I tend to disguise my discomfort in certain situations with humor. I don't take myself very seriously, but that doesn't mean I don't get a ton of shit done and execute better than most people.

The only downside to the dog walking business? I had plenty of dog friends but very few human ones. My boyfriend spent more time on the road than he did in San Francisco, so I didn't get to know any of his friends, which meant I had no support system when I discovered, nine months into my new West Coast life, that I was pregnant again. I was scared but determined to devote all my energy to this new project.

Dylan was born at John Muir Hospital in Walnut Creek, California, on January 23, 2015. Something I never thought would happen had happened: I was a mom. Up to this point in my life I'd been solely focused on myself. I wanted to have a successful career. How would this job or that job benefit me? What would I learn? What would I get out of the experience?

Having a kid changes *everything*. I wanted to be the best mom I could be. Brian and I talked after Dylan was born. "You should stay home with him if that's what you want to do," he said.

That's what I wanted to do. Who knew?

I couldn't wait to introduce my son to my family in Pittsburgh. When Dylan was twelve weeks old, the four of us—me, Brian, Dylan, and Peep—flew back east for a visit. As soon as I got there, I knew it was where I needed to be. I've come and gone from Pittsburgh enough times in the past twenty years that I've enjoyed a front-row seat for its transformation. Every time I come back, I notice how different it feels. I thought the big changes would have to stop at some point, but it keeps happening year after year. The city has become much more bike- and pedestrian-friendly, and the population seems to get younger every day. Now when people graduate from one of the local universities, they stick around instead of running off to New York or San Francisco. I didn't want to raise my son in one of those cities. I wanted him to be a true Pittsburgh "yinzer."

So I stayed. I left all my shit in California and settled down in Pittsburgh. I moved in with my dad and stepmom, but beyond that I had no plan. One day a month later, my dad woke up and said he was going to California to get my car. He was sick of me borrowing his. He immediately hopped on a plane, flew to SFO, took BART to Walnut Creek, and hailed a cab to my house. Then he loaded my car and was on the road heading east four hours later. In case you were wondering where I got my crazy, mystery solved.

Taking care of Dylan, I learned something new and amazing every single day. I watched him grow, change, and discover the world, all right before my eyes. He still amazes me but, six months into this new career, I decided I needed to do something else. I hadn't realized that babies don't actually do a lot of stuff. They mostly just sleep. Also, I had to carry him around for almost a year. Don't giraffes start running within minutes of being born?

If I was going to leave the kiddo at home with my crazy-ass parents and brother, I wanted to do something new and exciting, and I wanted to work with people who were doing something good for the world. I sent an email to a bunch of my favorite people in Pittsburgh and told them I was interested in working on something cool part time and wanted to get their thoughts and suggestions. On that list was the CEO of the Pittsburgh Parks Conservancy. "Let's talk," she responded. It pays to take the initiative.

I'd never worked at a nonprofit and was curious to see what it was like to be part of something that had a social impact.

There are a lot of things I like about Pittsburgh, but at the top of the list is the parks. I live just a few blocks from a 644-acre urban wilderness called Frick Park. This park is the main reason I chose to live where I do, so when I sat down with the Pittsburgh Parks Conservancy's CEO, I was all ears. She told me the organization needed a new website. They didn't have anyone on their team who was technical enough to manage the project. I helped them find someone who could develop the website and managed the project. I also worked with the team on content creation. It was an excellent part-time opportunity.

The more I was in the office, the more things the CEO wanted me to do. Could I help with this? Would I be willing to take a stab at that? Next thing I knew, I was overseeing communications and development and helping her restructure the entire organization.

I loved the impact I had on the organization, but I quickly realized that my skillset wasn't a great fit in an environment that was stuck in the past. They didn't use any of the tech tools I relied on so heavily in my everyday life, and the pace was slow. While nonprofit wasn't the right environment for me long term, I learned so much about how these organizations operated that would come in handy down the road. Sometimes you have to jump in and actually try new things to find out whether or not you like them. At the end of six months, I wrapped the contract.

A new idea was percolating in my brain, and I had to scratch the itch. I couldn't help myself.

CHAPTER TWELVE

Starting Another Startup

I'M ALWAYS COMING UP with really dumb business ideas. Always. I can't stop. I own a ridiculously large number of domain names. Every time I come up with one of these ideas, I call my ex, David Evans. He's one of my smartest friends. He's also very honest with me. The call always starts the same way: "I have an idea." Where it goes from there depends on the day.

"It's called Hood Wood, a subscription firewood delivery service for city residents."

Or: "Robot luggage shaped like a dog. When you walk around the airport, it follows you—and it's adorable."

Or: "Cat Tracker 2000. A cat door that tracks when your cat is inside or outside and provides a time log of its movements." (I still like this one.)

Nothing. Silence. He usually just hangs up on me.

Then one day, I called him and said, "I have an idea. I want to build an app that helps cyclists find the safest routes in and around cities."

"Hmm," he muttered. He didn't immediately hang up. That meant I was on to something.

I'd been an avid cyclist for years. I bought my first commuter bike after we moved the ShowClix office to downtown Pittsburgh. I was living in Lawrenceville at the time, a short, flat (rare for Pittsburgh) two-mile ride from the office. After spending a week sitting in traffic and paying thirteen dollars a day to park, I decided to get a bike. This was one of the best decisions I've ever made. I loved it immediately. Riding a bike made me feel like a kid again. I started biking to work every day. Soon I was riding my bike everywhere I went. I biked to have fun, get exercise, and explore new places. If I had free time, I was on my bike.

As soon as Dylan was old enough, I headed to Kindred Cycles in The Strip District to get the scoop on the best bike setup for the kid and me. I left the store with a new bike, a Yepp Mini child seat, and a tiny bike helmet. I couldn't wait to start cruising with my kid!

We started small. We'd ride around the neighborhood, visit the playground a half mile away, stop for pizza and ice cream, and then cut through Frick Park on the way home. There were so many places I wanted to go, but I couldn't figure out how to get there safely on a bike with Dylan. By myself, it would have been a different story. I'd been weaving my way through traffic in Pittsburgh and San Francisco for years, not overly concerned if I couldn't find a bike lane. I used my best judgment, and that worked for me.

I was far less confident in my decision-making with Dylan along for the ride. Even after spending years biking around Pittsburgh, I still had a hard time deciding which routes were the safest. If I was going to take my son somewhere new on my bike and feel good about it, I needed to rely on more than my best guess.

I was out for a ride with Dylan one day when it hit me. I always got the best advice from other cyclists, people who knew their neighborhood streets better than anyone else. They knew the safest routes, the shortcuts, the wormholes. Each of them was a fountain of ever-flowing local knowledge. Case in point: Aaron, the owner of Kindred Cycles. A few weeks earlier, I'd asked him how he biked his kid from Regent Square to the bike shop. His answer surprised me. I never would have thought to go the way he described. It also educated me. I'd definitely be going that way next time.

There's at least one Aaron in every neighborhood in every city. They know the best biking routes to and from nearly every neighborhood, and they love (or at least don't mind) sharing the inside scoop on them. I wanted to collect the expert knowledge that people have about their neighborhood roads and make it available to everyone, and I wanted to give people a way to provide safety ratings on the streets they bike the most. By working together, cyclists could help each other find the safest bike routes!

I stopped before I got too far ahead of myself. *Do bike safety maps exist?* I wondered. *Is that a thing?*

I went straight home and started my research. Google Maps does provide a layer for bikes, but the routes it suggested often dropped me on roads that I wasn't even comfortable riding by myself. The running, cycling, and swimming app Strava is for athletes. Everything about it was too competitive. Bike Pittsburgh, the local bike advocacy group, makes a beautiful printed map every year that highlights the city's bike infrastructure, but it doesn't provide information about *every* city road, particularly the streets that don't have bike lanes. Also, there was no chance I was carrying around a map with me. This wasn't 1980.

Where was the bike app for the commuter? The transportation rider? The "urban adventure cyclist," a name I'd taken to calling myself? How did this not exist?

I hatched a plan almost instantly. I'd crowdsource safety ratings on neighborhood roads from locals, build beautiful bike safety maps for cities, and help cyclists find the safest directions from point A to point B. My mind was spinning. I fell deep into a research rabbit hole. I was seriously considering building this tool. It could help so many people. I called it LaneSpotter.

As soon as I decided to go for it, there was no turning back. Just like that—and just like the first time—I committed to being committed. It was a very personal and ambitious mission. LaneSpotter would change the way cyclists experienced and moved through cities. The data we collected would be used to build maps that would make streets more accessible and safer to navigate by bike. The maps would encourage more people to get on bikes, help alleviate traffic, improve the environment, and make people healthier. My app was going to help make the world a better place!

I needed to see if my idea could actually be transformed into an app before getting anyone else involved. I wasn't an engineer, so I couldn't whip something up by myself. I'd also been a startup founder for ten years, which meant I was broke. I couldn't afford to hire someone to build it for me.

Then, a generous surprise. A year earlier Pandora had acquired Ticketfly, and Brian, Dylan's dad (and my now ex-boyfriend), had made some money from the deal. Brian knows me well. He knows I'm competitive as fuck and could tell that a mission was driving me. He could see the fire in my eyes. He was also probably sick of hearing me talk about LaneSpotter every time we hung out with Dylan together. He offered to help me build the MVP. Holy shit, I had an angel investor. Thank you, Brian.

If you're a nontechnical founder, you know that the most frustrating part of the process is not being able to build the thing you want to build. You *have* to get it out of your head. If you don't, you might go crazy. I'd been spending a few hours every night writing detailed specs and thinking about which features needed to be included in the MVP, so I had a good idea of what I wanted.

I looked for a dev shop that could do it for under $50,000. I spoke with five, but after my first call with a company based in Vinnytsya, Ukraine, I knew I'd found my team. My main point of contact was Inna. My project manager was Andrey. I was completely at ease with both of them from the very beginning. The language barrier was minimal. After talking through my idea for LaneSpotter with Andrey, I was confident he understood what I was looking for.

The product I wanted to build needed to test three assumptions:

1. People on bikes care about safety.
2. Bike commuters will rate the roads they travel to help other cyclists.
3. Cyclists want good bike maps on their phones and will use them for navigation.

Andrey introduced me to Vadim, Vasyl, and Denis at the kickoff meeting, and we talked through the specs I'd written. Once the MVP was complete, I wanted to be able to collect safety ratings from cyclists anywhere in the world. I'd use those safety ratings to create interactive maps that people would use to find the safest bike routes from one place to the next.

Every morning at eight, I logged on to Skype for our daily standup. My kiddo was by my side at the kitchen counter for every one of those calls. He was eighteen months old and acted his age. I typically maintained order by bribing him with small bowls of ice cream. It never got overly stressful because the team was so understanding. Despite the geographic separation, they got to know Dylan during these daily calls. He frequently popped in to say hello, and I never stopped him. He was my co-founder after all.

Working with this team gave me an energy boost every morning. They were subcontractors, but I could tell they truly believed in what we were building together. They sent me pictures of the incredible bike infrastructure they'd come across in Eastern Europe. These people were helping me make my wild idea a reality. I appreciated them so much that I shipped a giant box of LaneSpotter t-shirts and stickers to their office in Ukraine.

In just a few months they completed the branding and UI/UX work and built the MVP for web and iOS. They were fast, a result of the excellent process they had for managing the development. During that time, we didn't just talk work. We talked about our weekends, our hobbies, and our families. We connected on Instagram and Facebook. They became less like virtual friends and more like real ones.

While the dev team was working hard in Ukraine, I continued to spread the word to anyone on a bike who would listen. If you were a bike commuter in Pittsburgh, you did not want to get stuck next to me at a red light, which typically gave me just enough time to pitch LaneSpotter and request feedback.

This was really happening. I couldn't believe I was doing this *again*.

While the team in Ukraine was building the tech, I started thinking about how to take it to market with no budget. I reached back into my archives. The bike space wasn't as big as the event industry, but it did have something in common: an excellent segmentation opportunity.

When we first launched ShowClix, we weren't targeting anyone in particular. We were running general event ticketing ads on Google and taking what came our way. I wish that we would have segmented earlier, focused on a particular vertical such as museums or festivals. This time, I wasn't going to try to cater to *everyone*. I didn't have the resources. I needed to be more strategic about how I got this into the market. Segmentation was going to help me do that.

It's so much easier and cheaper to target smaller segments of the population. The four main types of market segmentation are *demographic, psychographic, behavioral,* and *geographic.* When it came to cyclists, the gold for me was going to be in behavioral and geographic segmentation.

Let's start with the behavioral. In my mind, cyclists can be broken down into a few categories, based on their riding behavior:

- Lycra-clad dentists riding $12,000 road bikes with their dentist friends on the weekends.
- Hardcore road warriors who log thousands of miles a year riding city streets and back roads. They're highly competitive and tend to use Strava.
- Commuters and transportation riders. They habitually ride their bikes to work or school and everywhere in between.
- Exercise junkies who ride to sweat, shed weight, and stay fit.
- Trail riders who spend most of their cycling time on a single track and rarely venture onto roads.
- Newbies. Some of these people own bikes. Others are bike-share users.

If my number one goal was to collect as many safety ratings as possible so I could build maps, I needed to talk to the people who were on their bikes every day. I needed to talk to bike commuters. They knew the roads in their neighborhoods better than anyone else did. They knew all the shortcuts. They knew which streets were the flattest and the smoothest, and which were riddled with potholes and should be avoided. They knew about the hole in the fence at the bottom of the hill that dropped you into a completely different neighborhood. They also really cared about safety and wanted nothing more than to see more people on bikes.

Next, I looked at the market through the lens of geographic segmentation. Most bike infrastructure is located in and around city centers. Cities are full of people who choose bikes over cars every day. To test my assumptions, I couldn't—and didn't want to—attempt a massive rollout. Instead, I decided to launch Lane-Spotter in two cities, get feedback, and then do a more significant push based on what I learned.

Could I segment the cities I'd chosen even further to gain maximum impact from my efforts? You bet! I made a list of the fifty largest metro areas in the country and created a list of questions that would help me get to know them better:

- Was bike infrastructure a priority for the city and its elected officials?
- Had the city installed any bike lanes or trails to date?
- If yes, were the city's bike infrastructure maps available online in GIS format?
- Did the city have an active local bike advocacy group?
- Was its bike ridership increasing by more than 50 percent a year?
- Was there a bike-share program?

My plan was to prioritize the launches based on how cities ranked according to these criteria.

When it comes to acquisition and storytelling, landing pages have always worked well for me. In almost every experiment I've run, the more specific and personal I've been when writing copy and designing graphics, the higher the conversion rate. Landing pages are cost-effective and let you test a bunch of stuff quickly, so I built a couple of city-specific landing pages that spoke directly to local bike commuters.

Throughout my time in tech, my marketing experience has been almost evenly split between B2B and B2C. I prefer B2B because it's more focused on building relationships and educating an audience than providing quick solutions and enjoyable content. While the LaneSpotter app was going to be a B2C play, in the beginning, my user acquisition model wasn't going to be. I was going the B2B2C route. I just needed to find the right partners.

But before I could do that, I needed to close my eyes and take a deep breath. I was about to hurl myself back into the early startup scene.

I knew from experience that this venture could lead me in all sorts of directions. I hoped for the best but was prepared for the worst.

This better work.

CHAPTER THIRTEEN

Being a Woman in Tech in PGH

ONE NIGHT IN 2017 I headed to the AlphaLab Elevator Pitch & Mentor Social. I'd grown to dread tech networking events in Pittsburgh. At this point, they were all just slightly different versions of the same thing. Nothing had changed since I'd launched my first startup. A decade later, the same handful of guys held the purse strings that founders needed to tug on to get funding. Yet I continued to attend these events because every founder needs a support system. Oh, and the free beer.

The founders who'd created the most successful, cutting-edge companies in Pittsburgh didn't come to these events. Very few of them were still active mentors. You can only give for so long without getting anything in return. The people who were the most dedicated to these events were the investors who had money to burn and the service providers looking for money to burn.

So I was surprised and delighted to see two new faces this evening. As I was working my way around the room saying goodbye after the pitches, two guys stopped me and introduced themselves. The conversation was still fresh when Bob sauntered over and butted in. This was the same Bob who, ten years earlier, after knowing me for all of two minutes, told me that Innovation Works would never invest in me.

It was a fairly normal networking conversation until Bob put his hands around my waist and said, "There's no way you have a two-year-old with a body like this."

At first, I wasn't sure I'd heard him right. Did he really just say that to me? And are those his hands around my waist?

He most certainly did, and they most certainly were.

This wasn't the first time something like this had happened to me. I was a woman working in an industry dominated by men. At a similar networking event five years earlier, the same guy had said to me, "Wow, you've lost a lot of weight. You should really only wear tight clothing now." But out of all the unfortunate experiences I'd had, this one was the by far the most mortifying. It was the combination of the comment about my body, the hands around my waist, and the fact that he'd involved my kid. Gross. The conversation immediately shifted from being friendly and jovial to awkward and uncomfortable.

I wanted to run. I wanted to cry. I wanted to scream. Instead, I shrugged it off with an awkward laugh and headed for the door. But the more I thought about it the more upset I got. I couldn't believe he'd done that to me, in front of strangers, at a professional networking event. Why didn't I say something right after it happened? Why didn't I speak up? That wasn't like me.

I'd sent a complaint to AlphaLab about Bob's behavior five years before and nothing had come of it, but that didn't stop me from submitting another one. I opened my laptop and sent an email to the team at AlphaLab, explaining what Bob had done and telling them I wasn't comfortable attending their events anymore.

This is what it was like to be a female tech founder in Pittsburgh in 2017. This is also what it was like to be a female tech founder in Pittsburgh in 2007. And in 2012. And it's the same way today. I've come to find out that I wasn't the only woman who had uncomfortable experiences at these events and that Bob wasn't the only offender.

A few months earlier, I'd completed AlphaLab's twenty-week accelerator program. While AlphaLab is ranked as one of the top tech accelerators in the country, it has been extremely slow to evolve with the pack. When accepted into AlphaLab's program in 2017, a startup received $25,000 in funding (not nearly enough), educational programming (mediocre at best), mentors (I'll get to this in a bit), back-office support (also not fantastic) and office space (vital to me). This, in exchange for 5 percent equity (way too much).

I didn't apply to AlphaLab because I needed the $25,000. Sure, it would have been nice, but it wasn't enough money to move the needle. I applied to AlphaLab because I wanted to work alongside other founders who were at the same stage in the process. I wanted to brainstorm with the other teams and leech energy and ideas from them. As a solo founder, I needed to get advice, help, and camaraderie wherever I could find it.

But that wasn't what happened. The vibe at AlphaLab was terrible. Nothing about it fostered creativity. I'd spent a lot of time at AlphaLab over the years. The two offices it occupied were colorful, vibrant, and well laid out, and the vibe there was exciting and fun—for the first few years. Then it slowly started to change, and not for the better.

By 2017, the offices were no longer filled with music, laughter, and ping-pong. They didn't even have good snacks or coffee. If there wasn't an event going on that day, you walked into a cold room full of silence. My cohort was especially quiet and small.

There was no energy in the space. Often the office was completely empty.

I should've realized that I didn't need AlphaLab to spark my creativity or further my connections. I should've just leased coworking space, identified the other weirdo founders in the office, and made myself at home. When the program ended, I left my free AlphaLab space and joined Ascender, a coworking space on the East End of the city. The office space was lively and filled with actual humans. Gwen made the best coffee and made sure I never had to listen to someone's favorite reggae album for an entire day. The biggest bonus? There weren't a bunch of creepy investors lurking around, making everyone uncomfortable.

Very little in the Pittsburgh startup scene had changed since I'd left for San Francisco three years before, but I certainly had. I was a little scarred and a lot more jaded, but I was also more experienced and confident. I felt like I was closer to being my true self than I'd ever been. I definitely wasn't myself toward the end of my time at ShowClix.

As ShowClix had morphed from plucky startup to corporate wannabe, I'd been forced to play a role I was never comfortable playing. Friends who've seen pictures of me from this time, with my long blonde hair, J. Crew dresses, and general neatness, call that version of me "Conservative Lynsie" or "Republican Lynsie." What a contrast to the way I look now, with my short punky hair, half-sleeve tattoos on both arms, and a bike hat perpetually on my head.

When I left ShowClix, I broke free from the shackles of caring what you might think about the way I look, and I have no intention of ever going back. I'm going to be fully myself from now on. You can take it or leave it.

* * *

I'd raised my seed funding for ShowClix at home. When I started to get serious about LaneSpotter, I figured I would follow the same path. I was excited to jump back into the startup community I cared so much about. Unfortunately, that community hadn't made as much progress as I'd hoped, especially on the investor side.

Here's a basic overview of the Pittsburgh investor ecosystem, which probably looks like the investor ecosystem in a lot of Midwestern and noncoastal cities in the United States. More than two dozen colleges and universities are located in and around Pittsburgh, including Carnegie Mellon University, the University of Pittsburgh, and Duquesne University. CMU and Pitt are the most active universities in the entrepreneurial community. They've helped bring more than a few amazing companies to life, and they're a great resource—for students and faculty.

Thanks to the generosity of two family foundations, both universities host prestigious startup competitions: CMU's McGinnis Venture Competition and Pitt's Randall Family Big Idea Competition. The winners receive anywhere between $5,000 and $60,000 in nondilutive grants.

The people who manage foundations like these are often angel investors as well. When they meet a founder they like, they invest personally. Some of them might take the next step and start an angel group, recruiting their wealthy friends to join them in their investing adventures. It's great to have this money available, but you won't get a ton of extra value out of these types of angel groups. They're smart, but they're not "startup smart."

After this comes the handful of series A funds in Pittsburgh, with the same people at the helm since their inception. For a long time, these few venture capitalists controlled the lion's share of the market, but that's starting to change.

And that's it. The VC funding in Pittsburgh basically stops there.

The biggest problem, and this won't come as a shock, is that there aren't enough women and minorities in Pittsburgh's investment community. The faces of old white guys in ties dominate the team page on virtually every single one of the funds' websites. If it weren't so sad, it would be comical.

The majority of the funding in Pittsburgh is seed-stage, and most of it comes from Innovation Works. Innovation Works is by far the most active seed-stage investor in Southwestern Pennsylvania, having invested nearly $65 million in more than two hundred local startups. These companies have gone on to raise more than $1.7 billion in follow-on capital. While it has an impressive funding history, what sets Innovation Works apart from other seed-stage investment funds (and not in a good way) is that it's a nonprofit, supported by the Pennsylvania Department of Community and Economic Development.

When Innovation Works launched AlphaLab in 2008, it provided a much-needed resource and solidified the startup community in Pittsburgh. The program helped make the city what it is today: a thriving tech startup scene.

There's just one problem: after AlphaLab launched, nothing really changed. The mentors are the same. The programming is the same. Demo Day is the same. The investors in the network are the same. The program plateaued.

In 2013, five years after AlphaLab was introduced, Innovation Works succeeded in mixing things up again by launching AlphaLab Gear. The hardware and robotics accelerator quickly became a nationally acclaimed program, thanks mostly to its smart, charismatic, and empathetic leader, Ilana Diamond. If only I'd met her a decade earlier.

Several times over the years, people from Innovation Works have asked me, "What could we be doing better to serve the startup community? What would you change?"

I've told them the same exact thing every time they've asked.

My answers will never change.

First, I'd love to see them increase the size of their checks and decrease the time it takes to receive them. The average size of the first check they give to a company is $50,000, and it takes *forever* to get it. Even though it's a convertible note, the paperwork required to get that check is cumbersome and requires a lawyer, making it a long, painful, and expensive process. To many, it's simply not worth it. I'm one of them; I'll never do it again.

I'd also like to see Innovation Works address salary disparity at the organization. Every founder in Pittsburgh whispers about it. The executives at Innovation Works make way too much money, and those who do most of the work don't make nearly enough. Like I said, Innovation Works is a nonprofit, so executive salaries are public. These six-figure executives expect founders to cut salaries to prove our commitment. Meanwhile, the president and CEO makes over half a million dollars a year. It's hard to trust advice from people whose actions don't match their words.

On the other side of the equation are the coordinators at Innovation Works, AlphaLab, and AlphaLab Gear. These are the people who make the organization go, the people founders love and respect the most. They tend to be women under the age of thirty, and many of them have been women of color. It's at this level where Innovation Works gets its diversity. These young women work long hours, do all the organization's grunt work, and make probably $40,000 a year. Compared to the CEO's bloated salary, such low pay seems unconscionable.

Innovation Works has always had a number of "executives in residence" on its staff. Executives in residence are typically former corporate executives, serial entrepreneurs, and angel investors who have enjoyed some success in their careers and understand how fucking hard it is to start a company. The idea behind the role is brilliant: invite experienced executives and leaders from established companies to work with startups for a year or two. In this role, former founders can serve as resources, mentors, and advisors in the startup community. With the constant rotation of fresh faces comes new networks of connections. This is how you grow a community.

There's just one problem: when someone lands one of these cushy jobs at Innovation Works, they never leave. Instead of being a source of cutting-edge advice, wisdom, and introductions for founders, these people seem more inclined to serve themselves. When founders began to criticize this arrangement, Innovation Works changed the title of the role to "portfolio executive," and with it has come a slight shift in how the position is viewed.

Startups and tech are about innovation and change. How can an organization support that sort of ecosystem when none of its executives has done any real work at an innovation-focused company in more than a decade? As founders, we not only want the people sitting across the table from us to look like us; we want them to be able to relate to us and help us during our journey.

If we aren't getting that sort of help from the staff, maybe we could get it from the mentor network? Nope. This one upsets me the most. Innovation Works doesn't understand the value of having a great mentor network. They've barely even tried. There are so many talented and helpful entrepreneurs in Pittsburgh who are willing to help, and the network gets even bigger if you maintain relationships with the founders who have left the city. Staying in touch with founders who have left would increase the size of the city's ecosystem exponentially. Just because we're not here doesn't mean we don't want to help.

And it's been like this forever. Being a woman in tech in Pittsburgh hasn't changed since I started my journey. The Pittsburgh investor ecosystem hasn't changed either, and as I learned the first time around, this ecosystem wasn't designed for someone like me. I was going to have to look for help outside my hometown.

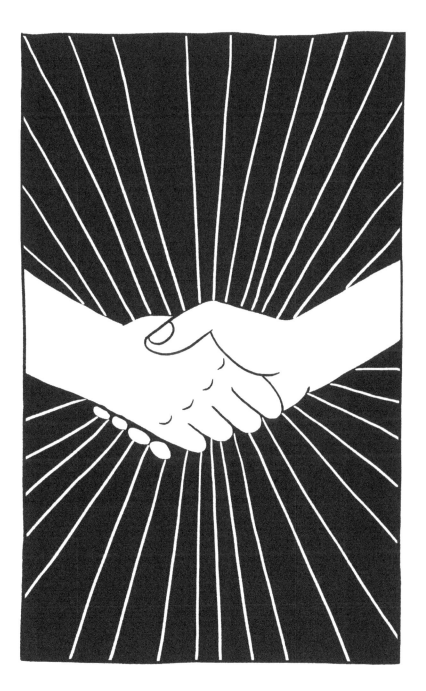

CHAPTER FOURTEEN

Building Great Partnerships

A T SIX ON a brisk morning in September of 2017, I headed north on Columbus Avenue toward Central Park. I was on my way to conquer the country's only all-urban hundred-mile bike ride: the New York City Century. Had I ever biked one hundred miles in one day before? No. Was I about to try? Heck, yeah!

I was in LaneSpotter's research phase, trying to learn as much as I could about how my partners were running operations, raising money, and engaging their members. I wanted to see how we would fit into this space.

I'd already spent a significant amount of time studying the biking communities in each of the cities on my list. Using geographical segmentation, I assigned each city points based on specific criteria. Obvious cities appeared on the launch list: Portland; Chicago; Washington, DC. Others surprised me: St. Louis, Minneapolis, Philadelphia.

Then there was the city at the very top of the list: New York City. Through efforts driven by a variety of different people and organizations, the city had invested a lot of money in bike infrastructure, which had succeeded in increasing the number of people biking around the city.

Some of those people owned bikes, but many didn't. New York's bike sharing program, Citi Bike, launched in 2013 and had been rapidly increasingly in popularity ever since. It helped that there were bike lanes and trails that could safely and efficiently transport you from one side of the New York City to the other.

One organization in particular deserves special credit for helping to improve New York's biking infrastructure: Transportation Alternatives (TA). For more than fifty years, this nonprofit organization has tirelessly advocated for better cycling, walking, and public transit for New Yorkers and successfully pushed for the construction of more than one thousand miles of bike lanes. They also helped bring Citi Bike to the city and were early adopters of the Vision Zero initiative. The organization has more than 140,000 members, and all of them love bikes. They're vocal and persistent, and they get shit done—the type of people I love to work with.

I reached out the folks in charge of TA and quickly got a response. They wanted to hop on a call so they could learn more about LaneSpotter.

I loved doing Zoom calls with bike advocacy groups. I didn't have an office, so I took the meetings wherever I happened to be working that day. My favorite place in Pittsburgh was the lobby of the Ace Hotel in East Liberty, a one-hundred-year-old YMCA building that had been stylishly renovated into a boutique hotel. Inside was a cavernous, three-story gymnasium, which I often used as my conference room. If it was an afternoon call, I might order a drink from the bar. My new bike friends appreciated the interesting backdrop and craft cocktail selections.

During my first call with the people at Transportation Alternatives, they mentioned that the New York City Century was coming up in just a few weeks, and they wanted to incorporate LaneSpotter into this event (and others like it in the future).

"Yeah, I saw that on your website," I responded as casually as I could. "I've always wanted to do that ride."

"You should come up for it! We could meet while you're in town and review your proposal in person."

"I'm in!"

Had I just committed to biking one hundred miles around New York City? Yup.

When I hung up the phone, I was all smiles. TA was progressive. They were tech-savvy. They had resources. And they had a team that was willing to try new stuff to advance the organization's mission. They were everything I wanted in a partner.

Unfortunately, every partnership call doesn't feel like this. If only every meeting I had was met with curiosity and an open mind. But I get it. The people in charge of these types of organizations get pitched all the time. *I* get pitched all the time. It gets tiresome.

I only wished I could have received as much enthusiasm in Pittsburgh as I got in New York. I was from Pittsburgh. I started my first company there. I'd been biking around the city for years. I really wanted to launch LaneSpotter in Pittsburgh, but when I started planning the MVP launch there, I didn't receive a very warm welcome. I introduced myself to the founder and executive director of Bike Pittsburgh, and we met for coffee. He wasn't dismissive of the idea, but he also didn't express overwhelming enthusiasm to help. It felt like he'd already heard what I was telling him many times before.

It didn't help that every year Bike Pittsburgh puts a lot of time, money, and effort into designing and printing a bike map, which our app would effectively render obsolete. They were willing to include me in a single email to their members, but that was it. It wasn't going to move the needle. I got a meeting with the City of Pittsburgh Department of Mobility and Infrastructure, but they were very meh as well.

One of the biggest chips on my shoulder is that I've never gotten enough support at home. I've always had to leave Pittsburgh to make any progress or gain any sort of recognition or success. For example, none of our earliest clients at ShowClix were from Pittsburgh—most of them were in New York, Miami, and Los Angeles. And now with LaneSpotter, it was becoming clear that to gain momentum, I'd have to look outside my hometown. Once again, I was going to have to leave my bubble to move my project forward.

It made sense to launch in another city anyway. Sean Ammirati, a former founder and current VC, suggested Denver. It was a super bikey city, and Strava was huge there. This could help me see if there was room in the market for a safety-focused bike app. I reached out to Bike Denver and got a completely different response from the one I received in Pittsburgh. They were beyond eager to get involved, and they had tons of thoughts and feedback to share. Much of their enthusiasm stemmed from the fact that they were a resource-strapped organization. They didn't have the money, people, or time to develop a mapping tool for local commuters, but they saw the benefits. They were in.

Then one morning, I was sitting at my desk without a ton of stuff on my to-do list. My calendar was almost completely empty. *Cleveland is only two hours away,* I thought. Something told me to reach out to the people at Bike Cleveland, so I tracked down their contact info and sent them an email. They got right back to me, telling me that yes, they were going to be around that day and that I should swing by and tell them all about LaneSpotter. I hopped in the car and drove straight to Cleveland—because somebody has to be nice to Cleveland. For yinzers, this joke never gets old.

Like Bike Denver, Bike Cleveland didn't have a ton of resources, but they did have a lot of enthusiasm. They were excited about being one of the first cities to get my app in front of local cyclists. I was blown away by how well the Bike Cleveland team introduced the app to its members:

> LANESPOTTER IS COMING!
> We're excited to invite Cleveland cyclists to take part in the pilot launch of a new cycling app called LaneSpotter! What is LaneSpotter? It's a web-based routing tool built to help cyclists find the BEST and SAFEST routes by bicycle. It will provide safety ratings on the roads you encounter throughout your day. As each of us inputs our ratings, the data gets better and better. It's real feedback, from real riders, and it's all local.

This introduction was so good I used it as a template for how other bike advocacy groups should talk to their communities about LaneSpotter.

The LaneSpotter story was gaining traction. People were excited about the idea and downloaded the app. They were adding safety ratings to the map. They sent me emails. They thanked me for creating the app.

I'm so glad I'd listened to my gut and emailed the team at Bike Cleveland. Everyone I met on the team was thoughtful and helpful, and the local cyclists were passionate. Within days of the launch, 350 cyclists had downloaded the app and added more than 1,000 safety ratings. It didn't take long, just a few weeks, before the biking community in Cleveland had built a map that stretched from downtown all the way to Akron, forty miles south. I took daily screenshots of the safety maps, tracking their progression and watching the ratings stretch farther and farther outside the city limits. I was so proud of what we'd built.

The bike community is a tight-knit group. Word started to

spread that LaneSpotter was out in the wild. Bike advocacy groups, community organizations, universities, and transportation departments started calling and emailing me. They were interested in promoting bike safety and collecting data.

After I talked to a lot of different bike advocacy groups, the picture started to become clearer. Like most nonprofits, these organizations operated on minuscule budgets and got most of their support from individual donors and a few small grants. Once I realized that, I began to understand that anything I asked them to do to promote LaneSpotter diverted resources from another effort. We needed to support the initiatives they'd already identified as being important in their communities, not add more work to their already full plates. How could a launch in their city be just as beneficial for them as it was for us?

I had an idea. We'd host something called The Great Rate, a weeklong contest across ten cities. Our challenge to cyclists: work together to create the most comprehensive bike safety map of your city. We'd invite bike advocacy groups to partner with us to launch the campaign in their cities. In exchange for their help with the launch, LaneSpotter would sponsor one of their upcoming events and give them free access to all the bike data we collected in their city. Win-win.

To encourage cyclists to provide safety ratings, I collected my favorite safety-oriented bike products to give away as prizes: Smith bike helmets, Spurcycle bells, and Nite Ize lights. The grand prize was an all-carbon Ibis Hakka MX gravel bike. These brands supported the mission. They were the perfect partner match.

By this point in LaneSpotter's evolution, the weight of being a solo founder was becoming too heavy for me. The effort it was taking to pull it off alone was taking a toll. I needed help, so I called a longtime friend who had tons of experience working in and with nonprofits, Dave English. Yes, the same guy we'd hired to sell at ShowClix—and then almost immediately had to fire. I'd learned from that experience, and this time around I brought him in at the right time.

To promote The Great Rate, Dave worked the phones and sent emails to bike advocacy groups, gauging interest and scheduling meetings. Meanwhile, I continued to work with the dev shop in Ukraine, created the marketing materials for our partners, and acquired everything we needed from brand sponsors for the ten-city launch.

If we were going to make this easy for bike advocacy groups, we had to create everything they needed to promote The Great Rate. I didn't want them to have to do *any* work. This would make it easier for bike advocacy groups to introduce The Great Rate, and it would also allow us to control the message.

When a bike advocacy group signed on to participate in The Great Rate, they got a kit that included:

- a link to a landing page customized for their organization and city
- email copy that could be used to introduce LaneSpotter and The Great Rate
- a link to a library of high-resolution images, including logos, prizes, maps, etc.
- a set of postcards to be handed out in advance of the launch

Not wanting to rely solely on the local advocacy groups in each city to launch, I created marketing campaigns to run on social media in parallel.

In our campaign to enlist ten partners for The Great Rate launch, we only lacked one, and it was the biggest and most important: Transportation Alternatives. So when they asked if I was going to ride in the New York City Century, I didn't have much of a choice, did I?

I committed to the NYC Century because I can't resist a good challenge. I also wanted to be the best partner I could be to these bike advocacy groups, and to do that I needed to experience some of the events they'd created. If I participated in the NYC Century, it would help me earn the trust of the team at Transportation Alternatives. I wanted them to know that I understood them, that I'd biked their streets and talked to their members, and that my app was designed to help them, not just my company.

The day didn't quite go according to plan. I crashed at the sixty-five-mile mark in Queens, hitting some metal edging that ran along the edge of a trail at the wrong angle. I went down *hard*. A few friendly riders helped me off the ground. I dusted myself off and made it to the next rest stop, where an EMS worker cleaned me up, covered the cuts and scrapes on my leg, and sent me on my way. When I finished, having ridden one hundred miles around New York City, I felt more like myself than I ever had before.

Shortly after entering Central Park for the post-ride festival, I ran into my main contact at Transportation Alternatives. He admired my battle scars and congratulated me for making it to the finish line. He also let me know that they were in for The Great Rate. We now had ten partners locked in for the launch. Boom!

As soon as we checked that box, I immediately shifted my focus to user experience. I didn't want cyclists to get dropped onto a blank map after they downloaded the app. I wanted users to understand what LaneSpotter was all about from the moment they opened the app. An empty map doesn't tell a story. A map with data does. The local knowledge was out there. There was an Aaron in every neighborhood in every city! It was time to partner with some local cyclists and add some color to our maps before going live.

Dave went on the hunt to find ambassadors. We needed people to add the initial safety ratings to LaneSpotter, attend local bike events, and be our eyes and ears on the street. Local knowledge was vital. Not surprisingly, it wasn't hard to find crazy bike people. We're *everywhere*. After we posted the job on Craigslist, the emails started rolling in. We scheduled Zoom interviews over the course of a week. It was so much fun talking to cyclists from different parts of the country. Everyone was excited to share the scoop on their local bike scene. They were equally excited about LaneSpotter and the impact it would have on that scene. City ambassadors received a LaneSpotter backpack, t-shirts, stickers, a set of postcards, and a paycheck. They worked hard to help us launch the app.

In October 2017, five months after our three-city beta test, we introduced LaneSpotter to cyclists in ten cities across the United States. Throughout the weeklong promotion, more than twenty thousand people downloaded the app and provided safety ratings on more than fifty thousand neighborhood streets.

We were gaining serious momentum, all thanks to the great partnerships we built with local bike advocacy groups.

Braving the Accelerator

I MADE A BIG mistake while trying to get LaneSpotter off the ground, one I promise I will never make again. For the first two years of the company's existence, I didn't pay myself. At the time I thought it was a selfless act that showed just how committed I was to the business. Only later would I realize how foolish it was. When I went to get a mortgage and a car loan, I was denied both because I had no recent employment history.

As annoying as that was, being perpetually broke was no fun either. Luckily, the universe intervened in the form of ShowClix's acquisition. I didn't dwell long on the fact that it sold for only $5 million more than the original offer Josh had been so offended by five years earlier. I was just happy to have some cushion. The timing couldn't have been better. I'd spent the past two years raising my son and building LaneSpotter without pay. With no steady income, things were getting dicey, to say the least.

As flush as I was now feeling, I couldn't say the same for Lane-Spotter. I was fresh out of AlphaLab's twenty-week accelerator program, and I'd used most of the money from the program on development work and The Great Rate. Cash was getting low. I needed to make some important decisions. How would I move the company forward? Did I really want to keep doing it all by myself?

When I feel stuck, lost, or confused, I either go for a long bike ride or take a few days off to be by myself, away from my house and the chores and the stress. In other words, I run away.

It was February and cold as fuck in Pittsburgh. I wanted to go somewhere warm, be outside, and, a rarity, do absolutely nothing. I wasn't even bringing a bike on this trip! I was trying to be more purposeful about my actions and the next steps I'd be taking. I was trying to be less impulsive, more thoughtful. I was trying to be smart. I was going to clear my mind and let my subconscious do the work for me.

I booked a room at a fancy resort in Southern California. It had everything I needed: good food, strong cocktails, a nice gym, and beautiful views. I spent a lot of time sitting next to the pool, reading books, and thinking. My mind continuously wandered back to my experience at ShowClix. *Do I really want to raise VC money again?* I asked myself. *Do I really want to risk my happiness and self-worth? Is anything worth that?*

No, I decided. It wasn't. After spending a few days in the sun, I knew I didn't want to raise institutional money. I couldn't stand the thought of having to deal with VCs again. The experience had made my life so miserable for so many years. If I went through that again, I wouldn't survive. I'd be permanently broken.

No, this time around, I was going to do it my way—once I figured out what the hell that was.

I returned to Pittsburgh and talked to as many people as I could about my options. Could LaneSpotter be a nonprofit? What would that look like? Could I merge it with an existing nonprofit such as People for Bikes? Were there transportation and mobility grants available for tech companies? Nobody had any advice for me. I should've kept asking. I gave up too quickly. I was impatient.

Instead of being more proactive and dictating LaneSpotter's next moves, I took a deep breath and waited to see which way the wind would blow. It came in the form of my very likable friend Brian Gaudio. I was invited to speak at an event at Ascender with two of my fellow tech founders, and he was one of them. I hadn't seen him in a few months, so I was excited to catch up before the event.

"Did you know that Logan from Techstars Chicago is in town?" he asked. "He's doing office hours tomorrow on the North Side. Even if you don't want to do another accelerator, you should meet him. He's a great guy."

Brian went through the Techstars IoT (internet of things) program with his company Module. Not only is Brian really nice; he's really smart. If he thought meeting Logan was worth my time, then I needed to do it. After the event I went home and checked my calendar. I had nothing exciting on my schedule for the next day. I checked Logan's schedule. There were still a few spots open. I booked one.

I had no idea the chain of events I'd just set in motion.

The day after the event at Ascender, I biked to a different coworking space on the North Side to meet Logan and Rachael from Techstars Chicago. Logan gave me some thoughtful advice and encouraged me to apply to his program. I could tell he liked LaneSpotter.

I started the Techstars application but didn't finish. I'd just done an accelerator. Did I really want to do another one? I'd also just decided that I didn't want to raise VC money. I was ambivalent until Logan emailed me the day before the application was due, encouraging me to turn it in. Sure. Why not?

I listed Chicago as my first choice and the Techstars Mobility program in Detroit as my second. The Mobility program sounded interesting. It was focused on helping innovative transportation-related startups. Among their corporate sponsors were Ford, GM,

Bosch, and Honda. With such a strong automotive influence, I wondered if it would be a good fit for a startup focused on bikes.

A few days later, I got a call from the Techstars Mobility team in Detroit. Would I be interested in learning more about their program? Again, why not? I hopped on a call with Ted Serbinski, the program's managing director, who, like Logan, I clicked with immediately. He filled me in on the details of the program. It seemed like a better fit than I was anticipating, and the fact that Detroit is only a four-hour drive from Pittsburgh was a huge bonus. Instead of having to fly back and forth to Chicago, I could drive.

The next thing I knew, I was on my way to Detroit for the in-person pitch. I arrived a day early to dick around the city, check out the breweries, and get a sense of the vibe. I immediately felt comfortable. Detroit felt familiar. It was Pittsburgh twenty years ago.

The next morning, I biked from my Airbnb to Ford Field for the pitch. I couldn't believe how many people were in the room! What the hell had I gotten myself into? I wasn't expecting to get accepted, so I hadn't prepared a ton.

The odds were stacked against me, especially as a solo founder. Paul Graham of Y Combinator goes so far as to suggest that out of all the mistakes that kill startups, having a solo founder is the biggest. Most of the top accelerators, including Techstars, warn solo founders that they're unlikely to be accepted to their programs. This negative view of solo founders has become so pervasive that it's extremely rare for any of the top investors to invest in a startup founded by a single person.

Making the hill I was climbing even steeper, I had no straightforward revenue model out of the gate. Every time I was asked about it, I fumbled for an answer.

I truly didn't expect to get accepted, so *of course* when my phone rang a few weeks later, it was Ted telling me I was in. It's so easy to forget your promises when an irresistible carrot is dangled in front of you. You always get what you don't want.

Shoving aside all the barricades I'd erected to avoid this path, I accepted the invitation.

I was proud of myself for having gotten LaneSpotter this far and excited about the opportunity and the challenge. I was also looking forward to getting out of Pittsburgh for a hot minute. A small town enveloped by a big city, its tech startup scene was starting to feel stifling.

My enthusiasm was tempered by the fact that I'd see my kiddo a lot less over the next three months. During the twelve weeks in the program, I'd be spending every Sunday through Thursday in Detroit while Dylan stayed with Brian. I hadn't spent more than a few days away from my son since the day he was born, and now I'd be limited to fawning over him Friday night, all day Saturday, and Sunday morning.

The days leading up to the start of the program flew by. I said goodbye to my friends over beers at Round Corner Cantina before embarking on the first of the four hundred-mile drives between Pittsburgh and Detroit I would take in the next three months. Nobody could question my commitment. I wanted LaneSpotter to work. I also wanted the validation, the respect I'd always craved but felt like I'd never gotten.

My life was about to completely change.

This is what happens when you say yes. Saying yes creates opportunity. Saying yes opens doors. Saying yes gives you options. Saying yes invites serendipity into your life. Most people think serendipity is accidental, like finding something you weren't even looking for. They equate it with good fortune, but I don't think that's true. Accidents and luck don't create serendipity; affirmatory action does. Serendipity starts with you saying yes to an opportunity. Accelerators are built on serendipity.

Techstars is really good at incorporating industry experts, knowledgeable advisors, and corporate partners into its programs. The first three weeks of every Techstars program is known as Mentor

Madness. I assume this is what fraternity hazing is like. More than two hundred mentors roll in and out of the office during Mentor Madness, and founders are expected to meet with them in fifteen-minute intervals, back-to-back-to-back, for a large portion of each day. They warn you that this is the most challenging and exhausting part of the program, and they're not lying. Every morning over coffee, I mentally prepared myself for what lay ahead. I reviewed the list for the day—names, companies, titles—along with my notes.

"Remember, it's not just about the person sitting in front of you," Ted would remind us at the beginning of each day. "It's also about who they know."

It makes sense. Everything is a numbers game. Two hundred mentors times one thousand LinkedIn connections each. You do the math. This is your new network. Treat them well, and they'll reciprocate. My network rapidly expanded, and as it did, I started to see different and new opportunities opening up over and over again.

In this environment staying top of mind is critical. When you're participating in an accelerator program, it's best practice to send weekly or biweekly updates to your mentors, advisors, and investors. It's also recommended that you start with your asks. What do you need most *right now*? Narrow the list down as much as you can.

During Techstars, my asks looked something like this:

- Looking for intros to VP+ level execs at REI, Bell, Trek, etc. If you know someone, hit me up, and I'll give you the details.

- I need to juice up my ASO knowledge. Is this in your wheelhouse?
- Have a good understanding of data-sharing revenue models? Tell me about it, and I'll buy you a beer.

Put your asks front and center. If the recipients of your email only have time to glance at it, these asks are the one thing they should see.

After sending just one update, I started to understand and appreciate the power of these relationships and the network I'd been building.

Whenever I sent an email with asks while I was in the Techstars program, it never took longer than four hours to get the intros, advice, or feedback I needed. That's fucking amazing. Mentors would hit me up out of the blue and say things like, "Hey, I just met so-and-so. It seems like the two of you should talk. Mind if I make an intro?" This sort of thing, getting relevant, helpful introductions out of nowhere, still happens to me *today*, and three years have passed since I experienced Mentor Madness. A friendly reminder about these update emails: don't forget to offer help or ask what you can do for your network. These relationships aren't a one-way street.

Most people think I'm extroverted. That's true—but only to a certain extent. If you let me loose in the right environment, surrounded by the right people, I'm fine. In those situations, I can effortlessly work my way around a room, albeit for a limited amount of time. The biggest challenge is getting me to the event. If I'm not speaking, I'll come up with every possible excuse not to go. I like to tell people, only half in jest, that the reason I have two dogs and two cats is that they give me an excuse to bail on things I don't want to do. My kid also helps with this now.

As an extroverted introvert, I probably appear to be having a great time at most events, but on the inside, I'm an anxious mess, and I get more and more exhausted as the seconds tick on. These experiences do not energize me. On top of this, tech, like music and ticketing, is a male-dominated industry, so most of the events I've gone to have been filled with bros. I've often walked into a room that had more than one hundred people in it and been the only woman there. These events are intimidating. I've always hated them, so I learned a survival technique and started gamifying them.

When I go to an event, I don't expect to close a deal, but I do want to have as many meaningful conversations as possible. My goal is to meet a few interesting people and try to connect some of the dots in my network. If I like someone I meet, we'll stay in touch and help each other at some point.

Working a room can be tricky, especially when you're looking to create a little serendipity. My trick: segment the audience! In 2011, I was able to weasel my way onto a ticketing panel at the Billboard Touring Conference in New York City. I'd be sitting next to Nathan Hubbard, the CEO of Ticketmaster. As excited as I was about speaking on the panel, I was not looking forward to the conference's big networking events, thanks mostly to the demographics of the crowd. In this case, music industry = mostly men.

As I walked into the first networking event, I scanned the audience and made a quick decision: tonight, I would only talk to dudes with beards. Facial hair segmentation! I (boldly and uncharacteristically) approached one dude after another, introduced myself, and said, "I'm only talking to dudes with beards tonight. How's it going?"

This trick worked like a charm. Not only did I meet a whole bunch of interesting people; I met their cool friends too.

While I was sitting in the lobby with our COO Tom Costa the next morning, every guy with a beard who passed by gave me a friendly hello! He couldn't help but smile. The tactic worked because I made it fun. The game I devised not only helped me get through the event; it facilitated several instances of serendipity. Remarkably, I still keep in touch with a few of the bearded men I met that day.

I felt uncomfortable heading into Mentor Madness, but those three weeks changed my life forever. It was just as challenging and exhausting as I'd been told it would be, but it was also fun—and very rewarding.

Now that everyone in the program knew each other, it was time to get to work.

CHAPTER SIXTEEN

Wearing Blinders

WHAT DID I actually do during the three months I spent in the Techstars Mobility program? I arrived with an ambitious plan. I'd mapped out all twelve weeks of the program, and I had three main goals.

First, I wanted to build V2 of the mobile app. I had a long list of things I was hoping to include in the next release, but there were only two things that absolutely had to happen. When we launched the MVP, the only way to create an account was by using Facebook. I got emails every damn day from people who wanted to use LaneSpotter but couldn't because they didn't use Facebook. V2 needed to offer more account creation and login options.

Due to budget and time restrictions, the MVP was also limited to the web and iOS devices. We didn't have an Android app in the beginning. At some point along the way, Cameron, one of the contract engineers I'd hired, started rebuilding LaneSpotter in React so we'd have an Android app *and* a single codebase. V2 would finish that project.

Next, I wanted to add a feature that would let me test a revenue model. As with lots of other apps, there'd be a free version and a paid, premium version. The main difference between the two would revolve around the number of routes you could save and the ability to share those routes with other users.

And finally, I wanted to launch V2 of the app in an additional twelve cities, including two cities in Canada.

That was the plan. Did I do any of that? Nope. Instead, I proceeded to make all the wrong decisions and ignore all warning signs. I wore my blinders so tight I'm surprised my head didn't explode.

Work on the product had slowed drastically since I'd ditched the dev shop in Ukraine. Bouncing from one engineer to the next wasn't working. This was one of the biggest mistakes I made along the way with LaneSpotter. Investors kept telling me that I needed an engineer on the team. A technical co-founder would be better. Nobody would take me seriously if I was working with an offshore dev shop. This was not true. I should not have listened to this advice.

I desperately wanted to find someone who'd be committed to LaneSpotter throughout my time in Techstars—and, ideally, beyond. I was stuck on the idea that I was going to magically find a co-founder/CTO who would swoop in and help take LaneSpotter to the next level. When one failed to appear, I posted the opportunity in all the usual places, emphasizing that the role would also involve participating in the Techstars program. I shared it with my network, but none of the people I knew had experience in this area.

Then, out of the ether, came a ping from Upwork.

His name was Chad. He was around my age, lived in the Bay Area, and had an impressive résumé. He'd worked with Mapbox, understood the tech stack I wanted to use, and was familiar with incorporating GPS into a mobile app. Perfect. Up to this point,

David Evans had vetted every engineer I'd hired. David had interviewed, hired, and managed dozens of engineers over the years and was nice enough to interview my candidates to make sure their technical skills matched what I was looking for.

This time, I took it upon myself to interview Chad first. We got on the phone and talked about his experience and my plans for LaneSpotter. I'll admit I was a little rushed and a little desperate. I wanted to hire the right person right away, and Chad appeared to be the perfect fit. He did a great job of selling himself, and I came away from the meeting thinking he was a guy I could connect with, an engineer I could work *with*. It's really hard to find engineers like that. It seemed like it was meant to be.

Chad showed me some of the work he'd done, focusing on the prototype bike app he'd built for Ford. That clinched it for me. Not only did the app roughly mimic what LaneSpotter aspired to do, but Ford was also one of Techstars Mobility's key corporate partners. The fact that Chad had done some work for Ford seemed like serendipity. I also felt like that connection might be useful if I tried to raise money or went looking for a strategic partner later.

Chad and I agreed to a four-month contract at $20,000 per month (San Francisco rates). Paying him would require spending half of the money I was getting from Techstars, but I was willing to do it to have someone sitting next to me who knew what the fuck they were doing.

During Techstars Mobility, Chad would get us to the single codebase, and because he was also a designer, he would polish the look of the app as well, give it a little extra something for the new launch. I'm a big believer in trusting people to do whatever they're really good at and not getting in their way. Chad was self-sufficient, so I'd be able to focus on building partnerships, connecting with sponsors, and working through the accelerator—all while hustling back to Pittsburgh every weekend to spend time with my kid.

Chad signed a contract with me about three weeks before the start of Techstars Mobility. I was ecstatic that we'd be getting a head start. On one of our first calls, we reviewed a to-do list I'd received from the people at Techstars. These were the things we needed to do before we showed up on the first day, and they included submitting a high-resolution logo, a company description, and a landing page URL for the cohort announcement.

As soon as I said, "landing page," Chad cut me off. "I've got it. I can whip something together in a few days." We didn't have a great landing page, so I agreed, even though I was more anxious to start the dev work.

A few days passed. No update. Then another few days. Nothing. I began to worry. "I'm almost done," he assured me. And then several more days passed. He finally delivered the link right before it was due. This small task had taken him *way* too long. I could've built a landing page in two days using Instapage or Squarespace—and I'm not a designer.

It's fine, I told myself. *He wanted to get the first thing right.*

But at the same time, in the back of my mind, I was thinking, *Fuck, I hope this dude isn't super slow.*

The morning of the first day of Techstars Mobility, I woke up in Detroit's Eastern Market neighborhood in an enormous, bright, open industrial loft I'd rented through Airbnb from a Russian guy named Vadim. Excited to meet the other founders in my cohort, I practically jumped out of bed and then hopped on my bike and pedaled the short 1.5 miles to the new Techstars office. We'd be the first cohort working out of a new WeWork building on Woodward Avenue, right in the middle of downtown Detroit.

When I walked into the office, I was immediately caught off guard. I was the *only* woman there.

In a blog post, Ted Serbinski, the program's managing director, talked about diversity:

The 2018 class is our most diverse class of founders to date. Of the 11 startups, all 11 startups have diverse founding teams in regards to *gender* [emphasis mine], ethnicity, or age. I'm incredibly excited to bring such a talented and diverse set of founders to Detroit for the summer. The teams come from all around the world, including Hong Kong, London, and across the United States. None of the teams come from Michigan.

Yes, the teams were diverse—in some ways. The gender split wasn't one of them. Fuck. There was only one other female founder in the cohort, Maya Pindeus, the co-founder and CEO of Humanising Autonomy. She and her co-founders split their time between London and Detroit, so quite often I was the only woman in the office. Calling this crew "diverse" was a stretch at best.

Honestly, the gender discrepancy didn't bother me at first. I'd grown so accustomed to it that I assumed I could easily overcome this hurdle once again. But I was wrong. I didn't connect with the other founders like I was hoping, and it wasn't for a lack of trying. It soon became clear that the other founders had no interest in hanging out with the only woman—and a single mom, no less—in the cohort. They didn't invite me to their late-night work sessions. I never had the opportunity to share my struggles with them and gain from their perspective.

My lack of connection with the other founders may have been rooted in the fact that I was the only woman there, but the office's layout exacerbated the problem. The WeWork space wasn't big and open like the Techstars office I'd seen at Ford Field, where all the founders worked together on the floor. At WeWork, the companies were forced to work in small offices, two companies per office. This sort of compartmentalized space lacked the collective energy typically found in an open accelerator space.

I ended up spending most of my time working in the common areas, getting to know everyone in the building except those in my Techstars cohort. At the end of each day, I went for a bike ride around the city. Sometimes I went with friends from outside the cohort. Bike people always manage to find other bike people. Often I went alone.

After Mentor Madness ended, Dave and I got back to work, and everything seemed to be falling into place. We formed several new partnerships. Bike advocacy groups were excited. Cities all over the country reached out to us. Interest was growing. The wave was building. During our calls, Dave and I were selling V2 hard, and in just a few weeks we'd lined up partnerships with twelve bike advocacy groups and a bunch of sponsors. Prizes were acquired. Marketing materials were created, and promises were made.

In addition to all the great partnerships we were building in the bike world, I was also developing amazing relationships with some of the mentors and corporate partners from the accelerator program. Eric Wingfield was my primary contact at Ford. A mobility strategist who focused on the future, he always gave me excellent advice, support, and guidance.

I also talked regularly with the team from Bosch Mexico. They believed there was a need for better bike maps and navigation in Mexico City, where public transportation was insufficient and traffic was spiraling out of control. On one occasion I had the pleasure of sitting across the table from the president of Bosch Mexico. He was French, had worked for Bosch in the Soviet Union during the Cold War, and wore a watch on both wrists. One of those watches was a classic gold watch and the other, a Swatch. Dave and I called him "Two Chainz." Two Chainz didn't just want to avoid the "bad roads" when he was on his bike. Two Chainz wanted to create bike rides based on the beauty of the route. This guy got it. I loved Two Chainz.

I also met Jake Sigal, the founder and CEO of the mobility software company Tome. Jake sold his first company Livio to Ford in 2013 and then launched Tome the following year. He has since built some of the most amazing bike-to-vehicle safety technology with some of the best-known bike brands and automotive makers in the country.

I'd found my people.

Everything was going exactly as planned—in Detroit. But I rarely, if ever, received any good news from the other side of the country. As soon as Chad started working on LaneSpotter V2, he came back with some thoughts. After digging into the code, he was confident he could build some of the additional features I had on my wish list. This work would be on top of all the other worked we'd discussed. Again, I believed in empowering the people I worked with. "If you really think you can do it, go for it," I told him.

Three weeks later, I knew something was wrong. I could feel it in my core. Chad was moving *way* slower than I'd anticipated. He hadn't shown me much of anything yet. I was expecting weekly demos, but every time we scheduled a call, he had a different excuse. The demo wouldn't load. The internet was down. Something broke right before the call. Sometimes he'd miss the call altogether, only to follow up later, claiming he'd been up all night working and slept in. He kept odd hours, he claimed. He was spending way more than forty hours a week on this, he claimed. It would still be ready in time, he assured me.

About six weeks into Techstars, I knew I was fucked. Chad was a disaster, and I needed to do something about it before things got even worse. In my mind, I had two viable options: get rid of this guy and try to find someone to pick up where he'd left off or push him even harder and hope he could deliver something—*any-thing*—by the end of the program.

Finding engineers had become the bane of my existence, so I never seriously considered the first option. This was a mistake. If I hadn't been so stressed out by the rapidly approaching Demo Day deadline and had been thinking clearly, I would have seen that I needed to move on. It was the *only* real option.

The goal of an accelerator is to help your startup grow, to gain as much traction as possible as fast as possible. Many founders lose sight of this amid all the networking and mentoring. At least that was what I did. I started making decisions for the accelerator—for Demo Day, not for LaneSpotter—and that was a big mistake.

I put my blinders back on and charged forward. I forged ahead with a stupid fucking plan, bullheaded determination, and fake optimism.

Fuck, this better work.

Optimism is nice, but accountability is even better. If I needed to hold Chad's hand until we got to the finish line, so be it. I logged into GitHub to check his progress, and what I found stunned me. Or rather what I *didn't* find. All of the code in GitHub was old code. MVP code. Chad had created a few repositories, but they were empty. Not a single commit. What the fuck?

I called Chad and asked him very directly what the fuck was going on in GitHub. This was not the question he was expecting, nor was it the question he wanted to hear.

"I'm writing the code in my own GitHub account," he said. "I'll push it over when it's ready."

"Okay. Can I see it? Can you show me a demo?"

Another excuse. And he was starting to get defensive.

I called David and told him what had happened.

"Something's not right," he said. "My gut's telling me that he's not doing the work. He's outsourcing it."

Everything I'd been ignoring for the last few months was finally becoming clear. I could finally see the cracks in the glass. Everything was getting ready to break. There wasn't going to be another launch. There wasn't going to be a V2. The guy I'd hired was completely and utterly full of shit.

My fury was building. I could barely contain the rage. After all the sacrifices I'd made, all the heartache and stress I'd endured, and all the tears I'd shed, my startup was in the same place it had been before I'd even heard of this accelerator program. I'd done all this work for nothing. I would have nothing to present at Demo Day, the culminating event where founders shared their progress and updates with the one thousand-plus people in attendance who were interested in working for, partnering with, or investing in our companies. I wasn't going to be able to share the story I wanted to tell. Instead, I'd be walking onto stage a failure. I'd failed to deliver on all the promises I'd made—to Ted Serbinski, to Techstars, to my investors, to my bike advocacy partners, and to the cyclists. I was embarrassed and so fucking pissed.

During the week leading up to Demo Day I was physically ill. My stomach was constantly upset. I was besieged by migraines, and I was breaking out in hives. Everything hurt. The reality of my situation was taking its toll on my health and breaking my heart. I had one weekend left until I had to stand on stage, smile, and pretend everything was okay.

I didn't want to spend my last weekend in Techstars sad and depressed. Rather than sitting around and moping, I decided to head north to Traverse City, a lovely town four hours northwest of Detroit with wineries, sand dunes, and the Lake Michigan shoreline. I was depressed, but I was still an eternal optimist. Putting some miles between me and Techstars gave me some much-needed perspective. The experience hadn't been a *complete* failure. The many connections I'd made during the accelerator program would shape my future.

The trip was only a temporary break from reality. As soon as I got back to Detroit, I sucked it up and reached out to Chad. There had to be a way to make this work. There had to be a way to compromise.

Unfortunately, he didn't have the same attitude. "I'm not showing you anything until you issue my last payment."

Was this guy serious?! I almost collapsed. Did he really think I was going to give him another $20,000? I hadn't seen a single working demo. I had no idea if he'd built anything at all. I had to wonder if he thought he could act like this because I was a woman. It felt like he was unwilling to compromise because he thought I'd back down. This asshole was confident he could get away with screwing me over, and I refused to just lie there and take it.

I dug in my heels and held my ground. "I'm not paying you until you show me what you've built."

"Sorry. I'm not showing you what I built until you pay me."

We went back and forth like this for a couple of days. There was no chance I was going to pay this guy. He was asking for all the money I had left. Negotiations stalled and then abruptly ended. There would be no compromise, only a stalemate that didn't help him but crushed me.

I thought it was over. I thought it couldn't get any worse. Then I logged into my GitHub account and discovered that Chad had done the unthinkable. Out of spite or malice, he'd deleted all my code. Not just the repositories he'd created, but the MVP code, the additional features that had been built, and the hacked-together React code Cameron had done.

Everything. All of it. Gone.

CHAPTER SEVENTEEN

Choosing to Fail

DEMO DAY CAME and went. It wasn't the worst thing that's ever happened to me, but it wasn't great either. All I really cared about at that point was getting home to my son. After twelve weeks of interstate commuting, I drove my dumb Prius, with my cat in the passenger seat, from Detroit to Pittsburgh one last time.

I then proceeded to do what seven-year-old Lynsie would've done. I picked LaneSpotter up over my head and smashed it on the ground. I didn't even have the strength or desire to look back and see where all the pieces ended up. I just left them there and walked away.

How the fuck did this happen?

I hadn't found a path to revenue that would allow me to sustain the business without raising money. When launching Lane-Spotter, I gave away lots of cool bike gear provided by a bunch of great brands. I'd spoken with the marketing directors for all these brands. Why the hell hadn't I asked them for money? They were already giving me shit to give away. My target audience was the same as their target audience. We shared a mission. Why didn't I ask them if they were interested in forming a partnership? How did I not see this as an option? Sponsorship dollars would have proven that LaneSpotter could generate revenue and that somebody was willing to pay me for all the work I'd been doing.

I had other options besides walking away, but I never fully explored them. The founders of the dev shop in Ukraine proposed an alternative working arrangement at one point: they'd provide free or deeply discounted development in exchange for equity. I loved working with this team, and it seemed like an interesting way to move LaneSpotter forward without funding, but scared that other investors might have a problem with the arrangement, I let the offer die on the vine.

I could have asked LaneSpotter's users for money and tried crowdfunding my way out of the hole I was in. I could have pursued grants, pitch competitions, or other types of contests. There are *always* options.

I definitely should have sought better advice, but I felt like nobody was listening to what I was saying. Or maybe they thought I was blowing things out of proportion or being dramatic. Perhaps they just assumed I'd figure it out.

I cut corners for Techstars that I wouldn't have cut otherwise. I obviously didn't vet the engineer I hired thoroughly enough. I was under a time crunch and wanted to get moving. Not having David interview him was another obvious blunder. And then, as Chad kept overpromising and underdelivering, I ignored it for the sake of pushing forward to Demo Day. I was desperate to have something to show at the end of the accelerator program. I made poor decisions because I had a rapidly approaching deadline and I was going to be on a stage in front of a bunch of people whose opinions mattered. If I hadn't been in Techstars when this happened, I would have cut ties with Chad as soon as I didn't feel good about him, but in Detroit I felt trapped. For the twelve weeks I spent there I was living in an alternate universe, and I didn't have anyone who could snap me back to reality.

I also didn't stay focused on doing one thing really well (as opposed to doing a lot of things fairly well). When I started Lane-Spotter, my goal was to collect as many road safety ratings as possible and build comprehensive bike safety maps for cyclists. The bike advocacy groups and city departments of transportation I was talking to started to influence the product roadmap. I started to build features for them instead of concentrating on accomplishing the goal. I added too many features to the app too soon. I wasted valuable time and money making a couple of features that nobody was going to use. I tried to please too many people. I tried to go too big. With nobody around to rein me in, my unruly, optimistic self went wild.

I was never completely candid with the people around me. I felt like I was asking them for help, but I never told them the whole truth. I'd been so self-sufficient my whole life I didn't know how to ask for the help I needed. I did tell Ted and my other advisors and mentors at Techstars that I was having issues with my engineer and that I was concerned about the lack of results I was seeing, but I failed to convey how concerned I was. Instead, I internalized it. I was simply too embarrassed to admit the urgency of the situation. I kept telling myself I'd figure it out until it was clear I never would.

Two months after Techstars ended, I continued to have conversations with several potential investors and my contacts at Ford and Bosch. Both groups were interested in finding a way to work together, but I knew it would be a slow crawl to the finish line with either of them. As big corporations, they did nothing fast.

What was the point anyway? The code for LaneSpotter was gone, and I didn't have it in me to fight Chad for it. Even if I'd wanted to, I didn't have the money to pay him or an attorney to get it. The episode with Chad was so embarrassing and scarring

I didn't want to mention it to any potential investors or corporate partners. It overshadowed all the progress I'd made and the success I'd enjoyed.

We've all been here, stuck in a downward spiral of negativity that feels like it has no end. *Why am I doing this? Should I be doing this? Do I even want to be doing this?* When it stops, you pick yourself up and start over. I'd ridden this crashing wave many times before, and I'd always bounced back.

This time was different. This was the moment I would have usually picked myself up off the ground, put all my energy into a new plan, and uttered my mantra: *this better work.*

I didn't do that this time. I walked away from LaneSpotter with more than fifty thousand active users on the platform. I walked away in the middle of two different M&A conversations. I walked away while getting daily requests from bike advocacy groups hoping we'd launch in their city. I walked away amid a constant stream of emails from cyclists thanking me for making biking in their city safer and easier.

I couldn't do it anymore. It was too much weight for me to carry with no funding, no technical support, and no co-founder. Let me be clear. I'm not saying I couldn't have done it without a co-founder, because I don't think that's true. I know plenty of solo founders who have been extremely successful.

But I did need help. I needed to find a couple of people to work with me who truly believed in the mission and vision. People who cared about the users and the product we were building for them. People who understood how valuable the data we were collecting was going to be.

I needed to find an objective advisor, someone who cared enough about me and my company to help me make intelligent decisions. I was too close to it, the same way writers get too close to the manuscripts they've written. It clouds your judgment. I certainly wasn't thinking clearly all the time. The weight was too much to carry, especially with a three-year-old son at home who needed me and who I needed more than anything else. It was time to choose happiness over heartache for my son and me. He was part of the equation this time.

Starting ShowClix had been hard. Really hard. Raising money from investors and navigating the ensuing relationships nearly destroyed me. But when I look back on this stage of my life, I recall the good memories first. I try to focus on the good and let go of the bad. But even if I couldn't see them or I refused to acknowledge them, the wounds were still there.

I didn't know just how deep they ran until I tried to raise money again. "Your reaction to raising money is similar to symptoms of PTSD," Ted once said to me. Hearing that didn't surprise me because that's exactly what it felt like—and to this day I'm still healing.

I was at a crossroads. I could fight to keep LaneSpotter alive and likely be miserable. Or I could put it to bed, learn from the experience, spend more time with my kid, and carve a new path forward without knowing where I'd end up.

The choice was easier than I thought it would be. LaneSpotter hadn't worked. I'd failed. It was time to shut it down.

"It's with much disappointment that I'm letting you know that I've decided to cease operations of LaneSpotter," I wrote on March 19, 2019, in an email to the fifty thousand cyclists who'd been helping me build bike safety maps for the last two years, as well as a few friends, investors, industry leaders, bike advocates, and journalists.

I proofread the email a dozen times. I knew I had to hit send, but I struggled to put the weight of my pinky finger on the return key. When I finally did it, I knew there was no turning back. I'd made it real.

Three days later, that letter—documentation of my failure—appeared in *Forbes* for all the world to see. "LaneSpotter Sidelined by Delayed Technical Improvements (For Now)," read the headline.

I should have felt sad. Instead, I was relieved.

It didn't work. I was done.

CONCLUSION

WHAT DO YOU do when the thing that was the center of your universe no longer exists?

I saw no path forward, no future. I had no idea what I was going to do next, but I did know one thing: I desperately needed a break and some space to think through what I'd just experienced. The end of ShowClix was filled with anger and frustration. This was different. When I shut down LaneSpotter, I was overwhelmed by sadness. I was so embarrassed. I felt like a failure this time.

Since I'm happiest in the mountains, I headed to Taos, New Mexico, for a weeklong ski adventure, where I immediately tore my ACL. Such is life. So instead of skiing, I sat in my condo, watching other people ski and thinking a lot about what I'd learned about myself over the course of my crazy career.

I knew that my experience was valuable and could help a young, eager team do great things, so the logical next step was to join an early-stage startup. I was ready to take a break from being the person in charge. I sent an email to my closest founder friends, hoping to unearth an interesting opportunity. If any group of people could understand my struggle and try to help, it would be my founder friends.

And then Jim Jen called. Innovation Works was restructuring, and they wanted to bring someone new on to run AlphaLab—and I was his first call. I was being thrown a lifeline for the first time in a long time. In the role, I'd work directly with early-stage founders, providing guidance and mentorship. I'd have the opportunity to reshape the accelerator programming, reengage the mentor network, and build partnerships that could help the entire ecosystem. It was the perfect fit, and it was exactly what I wanted to be doing.

After three rounds of interviews totaling eight hours, I got the call from Jim. "We decided that we're not hiring anyone for the role." He claimed budget issues. I've heard from people inside the interview process that the CEO Rich Lunak thought I'd be too "vocal." Rather than provide the lifeline, they drowned me.

I ended up accepting an offer from Ikos, a real estate tech company run by two of my friends, Steven Welles and Patrick Paul. I'd known them for years, having mentored them during their time in AlphaLab. Since then, they'd raised $7.5 million, and they had a team of fifty people but somehow no customer-facing tech. Other than the engineers, only one person on the team had actually worked at a startup. I knew I could help this crew.

During my first board meeting with the management team and investors, I asked the VP of engineering, Mike Schenck, why the tech was so far behind. I didn't think anything of it when I posed the question. Maybe I could've worded it better, but I was genuinely curious as to why they hadn't built anything for their customers yet, why all the development work had been devoted to internal tools. The backlash was immediate and severe. From that day forward, Mike made sure I was never invited into the room to talk through big technical decisions with him and the founders. During the year I spent with the company, this guy harassed me so much that I had to file two formal complaints against him. The complaints were more than justified and, given his history, not surprising. In his previous job at Uber, his team had been written up publicly for harassing female software engineers. This shit never ends. And it's everywhere.

While Ikos wasn't the experience I was hoping for, it succeeded in driving me back into the startup scene. I decided to transition into full-time consulting for early-stage tech companies. A few consulting gigs led to a contract with a fintech incubator in Pittsburgh called numo. I stuck around for nine months, working on a banking solution for gig workers. I ended up doing a lot of entry-level marketing work. During this contract, I realized if I was going to join somebody else's startup, I needed to be in a senior-level position. I'm incapable of sitting back and watching. I have to be in a position where I can fix problems and drive change. I need to be in a role where my voice will be heard.

And then two things happened in 2020 while I was writing this book.

First, in July, Ying-Tsao Tan, the founder of Electric Momentum, emailed me from Paris. He wanted to talk about LaneSpotter and see if there was an opportunity to work together. As much as I hated reliving the story, I agreed to hop on Zoom and talk. "The code's gone," I explained. "There's nothing I can do." A couple of weeks later, he scheduled another meeting to follow up. He had more questions. He had ideas. Ugh. I couldn't stop thinking about LaneSpotter and the original mission and vision. I still cared so much. I still wanted it to work.

And just like that, he'd awakened something that had been dormant in me. He'd poked the beast.

I reached out to GitHub, and this time someone responded, *and* they were able to get me into my old account. When I logged in, staring back at me was LaneSpotter's original MVP code. I have no idea how it reappeared, but it did, so I kept digging. Upon further investigation, I discovered that I still had *25,000 active users* on the busted app, and the 160,000 safety ratings I'd collected after the ten-city launch were still stored in Mapbox. It was enough to reignite the fire.

Could I resurrect this thing? Could LaneSpotter exist again?

I shared my desire to resurrect LaneSpotter with my friend Grant Gillman, who I'd met while working at Ikos. The more we talked about it, the more he demanded I give it a shot. And not by myself this time; he wanted to help. He wanted to join as a co-founder. Shortly after that, I reconnected with a woman I met while working at numo, Anna Lawn, a super talented UI/UX researcher and designer. She saw something in LaneSpotter, and she wanted to help too.

If I was going to attempt to resurrect LaneSpotter, these were exactly the people I wanted by my side. At the start of 2021, Grant, Anna, and I started spinning up a new and improved LaneSpotter.

People have asked, "Why put yourself through this again?" I'm giving LaneSpotter another go not because I want to torture myself but because I want the chance to do it right for once. We built a great company with ShowClix. The company continues to grow and thrive, but I didn't get to do it the way I wanted to. And, of course, my original experience with LaneSpotter was disheartening, to say the least.

I'm confident my second stab at LaneSpotter will be much better than the first, thanks to my new co-founders. They understand and support my strengths. "Anna and I were talking last night, and we've decided that we need to set you loose," Grant recently said to me. "Let us build the product. Let us run things. You go and do what you do. Connect the dots and kick down the doors for us. It's what you do best."

Grant's right. While I'm more than competent on the operational side, my biggest strengths are more visionary and relationship-based at this stage of my career, and I'm okay with that. I'm good at it, and it makes me happy. Why wouldn't I do what makes me happy?

The second thing happened in October of 2020. Ted Serbinski, my friend and former managing director at Techstars Mobility, called to pitch me an idea. He wanted to launch a seed-stage venture fund in the Midwest—and he wanted me to be involved. I'd never considered sitting on the other side of the table. If you would've told me I'd be a venture capitalist one day, I would have said, "No chance in hell."

This was different, though. We wouldn't be launching a traditional venture capital fund. Our fund would be an expansion of The Fund, a seed-stage venture fund originally launched out of New York City by two very successful startup investors, Jenny Fielding and Scott Hartley. The concept was simple but powerful: assemble the most successful founders in a city and start a fund to invest in the next generation of local entrepreneurs. Their success in NYC led to fast expansions into London, Los Angeles, and the Rockies. Ted had signed on to assemble the team that would run The Fund Midwest.

I didn't see this one coming. Becoming a venture capitalist was not on my list of things to do, but that didn't dissuade me from doing it. In fact, I immediately recognized the impact I could have in this role, so I signed on as a general partner of The Fund Midwest. I'm a VC now.

One of the reasons I was so excited to join The Fund is that it's a "founders fund" composed entirely of entrepreneurs looking to help other entrepreneurs. Our goal: to be one of the fastest first-check writers in the Midwest. We'll make two investments of between $50,000 and $100,000 each in early-stage companies in the Midwest every month for the next two years.

Another reason I was excited about this opportunity is that as part of its mission, each of The Fund's investment committees has to be gender-balanced, with two men and two women making the funding decisions. The investment committee for The Fund Midwest follows that mandate. We have Ted Serbinski in Detroit, Jennifer Fried in Chicago, Chris Bergman in Cincinnati, and me in Pittsburgh.

While venture capital boomed in 2020, only 2.2 percent of VC money went to women. Meanwhile, across The Fund's entire portfolio, 45 percent of the companies we've invested in have a female or minority founder. Now that's shaking shit up.

Once I was begging for money from VCs who were as different from me as possible. Old white guys in ties. Now I'm a VC, which means I have the opportunity to create real change from the other side of the table.

All I ever wanted was for somebody investing in me to look like me, and now I can be that person for other female founders. It feels almost implausible because I know what it's like to be overlooked, excluded, even ridiculed simply because of my gender. I also know that my presence at the table is what these female founders need more than anything else.

* * *

I wrote this book for my fellow female founders. I needed to shed light on the inequality that's so pervasive and corrosive in our industry. I needed you to know that you're not alone. Now, besides speaking out against the problem, I can do something even more tangible. I can write checks to people who look like me, and that feels incredible.

After lots of ups and downs and several head-on collisions, my curvy, chaotic, and unpredictable journey has finally come full circle.

And this time, I think it's gonna work.

ABOUT THE AUTHOR

Lynsie Campbell is the founder of two tech companies: ShowClix and LaneSpotter. One was acquired. The other, not so much. She's also one of the general partners of The Fund Midwest, a seed-stage venture fund investing in the next generation of tech founders. Before tech, Lynsie worked in the entertainment industry, doing stints at *The Rosie O'Donnell Show* in New York City and as a music publicist in Los Angeles. Her work has appeared in NPR, CNN, *Forbes*, *Billboard*, and *WSJ*. Lynsie was born and raised in Pittsburgh, Pennsylvania, and currently lives there with her son Dylan, two dogs, two cats, and seven bikes. To connect with Lynsie, visit www.lynsiecampbell.com.